Yep...
I'm a
Medium

Cheryl S. Kearns
with Lacey Matthews

Copyright © 2019 by Cheryl S. Kearns

All rights reserved

ISBN 9781091448001 (paper)

No part of this book may be reproduced, scanned, or distributed in any printed or electronic form without permission. Please do not participate in or encourage piracy of copyrighted materials in violation of the author's rights. Purchase only authorized editions.

It is not the intent of the author to give any professional advice, medical or otherwise. The author's intent is to share her experiences and knowledge in a general nature to help you on your spiritual, emotional, or physical journey. The author assumes no responsibility for your use of said techniques or actions taken by you.

Contributed stories printed with permission

Book and cover design by Melanie Miller

Cover background photo by Lacey Matthews

I would like to dedicate this book to Leo Alfano and all of the Spirits that have been so kind to let me channel their messages! It has been through you that I have found my greatest healing and growth!

I want to also dedicate this book to my daughter Lacey for taking this journey with me and being my sidekick as Inner Harmony Mediums in delivering these healing messages!

And last, but not least, I dedicate this book to my husband who has always believed in me and encouraged me to "do what I do!" My Rock, Ben!

Leo Alfano (Photo courtesy of the Alfano Family)

FOREWORD

Leo Alfano

by Lacey Matthews

Mom and I felt compelled to share with you a little bit of our journey as Intuitive Mediums! With the consent of the Alfano family, we would like to share with you how our lives changed and, life as we know it now, came to be—all because of an AMAZING ANGEL named Leo Alfano!

We have been blessed with a "gift" that we never expected! This journey started many years ago and possibly at birth. As most children do, we turned our gifts off at some point in our childhoods. Mom probably turned it off due to difficult situations as a child and I probably due to being scared by these gifts at some point during my childhood. Children are usually very "tuned in" because of coming from the Other Side not long ago, but we either decide to use and develop our gifts or we choose to turn them off. For reasons we may never fully know, we both turned them off at certain points during our childhoods. During our adult years, these gifts started showing themselves again!

Mom decided to tackle her childhood adversities and, therefore, started using her gifts again! She soon realized she could help cross Spirits over to the Other Side and things just blossomed from there. Mom welcomed her gift and started using it again. For her, talking to the dead and helping them became a normal daily activity. But she held back from revealing this gift to very many people due to knowing in a small town it would come with a lot of ridicule. But everything changed in July, 2013 because of Leo Alfano!

I, on the other hand, never thought I would use my gifts and I definitely didn't view them as "gifts." I always knew when a Spirit was close and I would refuse to look in a certain direction or area because I knew what I would see. I was hiding from my gift and completely planned on keeping things that way until Leo turned life upside down.

On the morning of July 18, 2013, life as Mom and I knew it changed forever after Leo Alfano was in a fatal motorcycle accident. Leo was 19 years old and the sweetest young man you would ever meet. He lived life to the fullest with a smile always on his face. The questions of "why" started to surface. Why did this have to happen? Why to such a young man? Why to such a bright Spirit? Why, Why, Why? "Why" might never be answered except that it was his time. Leo truly LIVED life in the short time he was here. He touched so many lives in this small town and is still touching lives from the Other Side. He was an Angel on Earth! How does a family get through a loss like this? No parents should ever have to bury their child. No brother or sister should have to feel the pain of losing a sibling so young. How do you help them get through it? There are no words or gifts or actions that will make it hurt any less. What do you do? Ironically, we found out the answer to that question from Leo himself!

Leo was an Angel among us on earth. There are very few people who could impact the number of people's lives that he did. He blessed his family, friends, and community, even if it was just for a short while. Now, he is continuing to impact people from the Other Side. The impact of his passing affected so many people. This is where our journey truly began. Leo is a very strong Spirit and many have seen that in the short time since his passing. He began reaching out and comforting his family immediately.

He first reached out to me less than 48 hours after his passing. You have to understand he did this because I would never have asked or wanted to receive messages from the Other Side—so these messages were more impactful. He first showed himself to me as a reflection in a balloon. He was standing behind his brother Peter with his hands resting on Peter's shoulders in comfort. Then later that day, Leo appeared to me and wanted messages delivered to his family! You can imagine my surprise as this is the last thing I would have wanted or expected and even thought I might have made up the entire conversation. Leo said, "Please tell my family that I love them and will always be watching over them!" I am sure at this point you can imagine just how crazy I thought I was. I was talking to a Spirit and could hear him as if he were physically there. He then clapped his hands together, which he relayed meant his passing was quick and without suffering. He then took off what appeared to be a gold chain necklace with a gold cross on it. His mother Tonia flashed in my mind and I knew he wanted this necklace given to her. I was in utter shock and disbelief and wasn't even sure if I ever planned on telling anyone about this experience. Mom and I are VERY close and I did tell my experience to Mom who was starting to really embrace her own gifts. Mom remembered seeing Leo wearing a gold cross necklace at Leo's Pizza the day before his passing. That was confirmation enough for us that we had to tell his family these messages. But we both decided to wait until after the funeral. Clearly, Leo had other plans!

He started turning lights on and off, making the back of a toilet fill with water when it hadn't been flushed, and so on. So we knew it was important to Leo for these messages to be delivered immediately! I was still uncertain of my gifts and worried the Alfanos wouldn't believe me, or worse, it would somehow cause them more pain. So Mom made a phone call to Tonia to tell her about these messages and what was confirmed was unbelievable! Tonia said Leo had a favorite gold chain necklace and she was struggling with keeping it or burying it with him. She stated she hadn't told ANYONE about the necklace and her struggles with what decision to make. Her husband Sam also confirmed these messages and stated one of his biggest concerns was whether Leo's death was quick and if he had suffered. Leo knew exactly what his parents needed at that time to bring them some comfort! These messages somehow brought this family some sort of peace during this devastating tragedy. In the days, weeks, and months to follow Leo's passing, he has not only connected with Mom and me with messages for his family, but he also very quickly started bringing his family messages that he knew they would see.

An Angel is the only way Leo can be described and that somehow doesn't even do him justice. Leo easily connects with his sister Filie through dreams and in ways that only a little brother could get away with. He is constantly there with those supporting hands on his brother Peter's shoulders. He always lets his mom and dad know when he's around with feelings, sounds, moving objects, and so much more!

But Leo wasn't finished with Mom and me just yet. He came to Mom and told her that she had to start offering her gifts to everyone. He told her she had to follow her dreams and write this book. He visits her on a regular basis with messages and has even stepped in as a Spirit Guide for the time being. He loves to startle me and refuses to let me hide from my gifts any longer. Because of Leo and the entire Alfano family, Mom and I knew that we had the support we needed to jump off the ledge and start offering the gifts we have been blessed with to everyone. He is always present when we do readings (especially group readings) and he encourages and guides us on a daily basis. He showed us the peace, comfort, and healing that loved ones feel when they connect and receive messages from their loved ones on the Other Side. Leo pushed Mom and me into offering this gift to others who are suffering in similar ways. He helped make all of this possible and gave us the push we needed (and still need at times) to be strong enough to stand out on the ledge and know it will all be okay.

This is a small town and this gift won't come without some ridicule, but because of this beautiful amazing Angel, we have the support and comfort to actually start helping people heal. We are all put on this earth to help one another and we could all learn so much from Leo. As one friend said, "We should all be more 'Leo-like!'" Leo, we love you and thank you for giving us the push that was needed and for continuing on a daily basis to give comfort, support, and amazing messages. We are honored beyond words that we were and still are able to share Leo's messages. Please share this with your friends and family so they, too, can find comfort in knowing their loved ones are with them all the time. Maybe they also can find some peace and comfort from receiving messages from their loved ones on the Other Side.

Spirit is amazing and with Leo, our Spirit Guides, Angels, and God helping us, our journey is going places we have never dreamed. So our journey continues to grow and on a daily basis it continues to amaze us. Spirit is amazing and we love every reading we are able to do. I will never again "hide" from my gift, Mom will openly share it with everyone without worry, and we will try to help as many people as possible. We hope this has helped give some comfort to those of you reading this and has shown you a small part of how Spirit communicates. Please know your loved ones watch over you every day and are eager to connect and comfort you. This is the beginning of our journey as Inner Harmony Mediums!

Photo by Lacey Matthews

INTRODUCTION

What did you want to be when you grew up? I just knew I wanted to "help people." Never in a million years would I have guessed that my Life Purpose would be me talking to Spirits that have crossed over to the Other Side! The fact that my daughter Lacey and I would be delivering messages from the Other Side to help heal people's Souls was never in my wildest dreams!

Two days after my friends' (the Alfanos) 19-year-old son Leo passed in a motorcycle accident, he came through and said, "You are going to do readings and write a book!"

I thought he was crazy! There was no way I was doing that! I'm from a small town, with a small business. Nope . . . no can do!

You will find out in the pages to follow that Leo won this debate! I thank him and my entire Spiritual Crew on the Other Side for pushing us over the Spiritual Cliff, so to speak.

The beautiful stories you are about to embark on will change your life, just as they have changed Lacey's and mine. I am grateful beyond words to all of the Brave Souls on this side and the Other Side for sharing their lives and stories with all of us. May the healing begin!

Photo by Lacey Matthews

ACKNOWLEDGMENTS

You have always heard it takes a village, and this is so true in writing this book.

First of all, I want to thank my friend and Spirit Guide Leo Alfano! When you gave my nine-year-old grandson Malik the message, "Tell your Nana she needs to do readings," and then you came to me and said, "You're going to write a book!" I thought you were crazy. Well, here it is and I hope I didn't disappoint!

I want to thank every Spirit that I have ever had the pleasure to work with and also those yet to come.

How can I ever thank my teachers enough? The valuable lessons that I have learned from Rod Stryker and Raymon Grace are priceless. Also, thank you to all of the teachers through my life journey. Here's to the next chapter of lessons to come.

A big Thank You to my daughter Lacey! Without you, there wouldn't be Inner Harmony Mediums. I look forward to you and I delivering many more healing messages. I love you to the moon and back!

Thank you to Sam, Tonia, Peter, and Filie Alfano for your love and support and for opening your hearts and Souls to me. You will always be family to me!

Thank you to all of you who were kind enough to share your stories for this book. You have no idea how many Souls you are going to heal. Lacey, Malik, and Nevaeh Matthews; Cathy Reichert; Jared and Rachel Leake; Sam, Tonia, Peter, and Filie Alfano; Apryl Edwards; Lisa

Winnett; Judene Stock; Sharon Kassing; Debbie Pettit; Joyce Coates; Paula Kloker; Debbie Springman; Lilly Costello; Deb Davis; Michelle Thomas-Vogel; Loren Hamilton; Jennifer Barrett; Susan Hartley; JoAnn Chumley; Deb Kunz; and Todd Williams.

To all who proofread and edited my book before it went to print, your hours and dedication are priceless: Lacey Matthews; Cathy Reichert; Kylie Crabtree; Allison Tucker; and Michele Rush—and my final editor, Melanie Miller.

A special thanks to Melanie Miller for her extreme talent and patience while designing and editing my book and creating our portraits. Also, huge praises to her for the beautiful cover she designed. A special thank you to Lacey Matthews for the nature photography on the cover and throughout the book.

A huge thank you to Kylie Crabtree for pouring countless hours into deciphering my handwritten book and typing it up as she kept my business running. This translation was a hot mess!

Special thanks to my honest friend, Cathy Reichert, for her endless hours of helping me on the layout and complete honesty as she listened to my stories again and again. Trust me, she's honest. I love you friend!

CONTENTS

                                                                                                    Page

Foreword: Leo Alfano by Lacey Matthews v

Chapter

1. STEPPING INTO THE LIGHT 3
    The Red Telephone 3
    Introduction to Debbie P's Story 3
    Debbie P's Story 4
    The Screwdriver 8

2. MY LIFE 11
    About Me 11
    My Childhood Memories 13
    What is Your Life Purpose? 15
    You Can't Force Life 17
    Ten Talents 18
    Answering the Call 18
    Moving Away from Negative People 19
    Letting Go 20

3. EVER CHANGING 23
    Something Unpredictable 23
    So, You're a Witch? 30
    Deb D's Story 32
    JoAnn's Story 33

4. FOR THE LOVE OF LEO 37
   Journaling 37
   Introduction to Tonia's Story 38
   Tonia's Story 38
   The Contract 44

5. SPREAD YOUR WINGS 47
   Lacey's Story 47
   The Process 52
   Readings 53

6. HEALING VISITATIONS 55
   Sam's Story 55
   Ambassadors 59
   Peter's Story 60
   Filie's Story 63
   Who am I Really? 68

7. PAYING ATTENTION 71
   Spirit Talks to Us in Many Forms 71
   Michael 72
   Angelic Music 73
   Pay Attention to the Signs 74
   Joyce's Story "Drops of Jupiter" 77
   Penny for Your Thoughts (Joyce) 83

8. HEALING THE WOUNDED SOUL 85
   Feeling Desperate 85
   Paula's Reading 86
   Susan's Story 89
   Sharon's Story 92

9. HEAVENLY CONNECTIONS 97
   Archangels 97

	Archangel Michael 98
	Seven Archangels 98
	Spirit Guides 100
	Spirit Guide Legend 103
	Cathy's Story 105
10.	REFLECTIONS OF THE SOUL 107
	Faith 107
	Michelle's Story 107
	Debbie S's Story 109
	Debbie's Granddaughter's Story 110
	Jen's Story 112
11.	GIFTS FROM HEAVEN 115
	Judene's Story 115
	Lisa's Story 120
	Whitening Toothpaste 124
	911 125
12.	A SOUL'S BLUEPRINT 127
	Soul to Soul Connections 127
	Partners in Crime 128
	My Dharma Code 129
	Dowsing 132
	Soul Channeling 135
	My Visitation Dream 137
13.	GHOST ... SPIRITS ... WHAT? 141
	Loren's Story 141
	Williamson Funeral Home on Sandy Street 143
	Spooning 146
	Plain Jane 147
	Hardin Salvage Yard and the Alton Bridge Backwater 148
	Savannah, Georgia 149

14. BE EXTRAORDINARY 151
    My Kids and Spirits (by Lacey Matthews) 151
    An Interview with Malik: Meet His Spirit Guides 155
    An Interview with Nevaeh: Meet Her Spirit Guides 157
    Lacey Teaching 157
    Out of the Mouths of Babes 158
    My Grandkids "Dance Recital" 159
    Spirit Through a Child's Eyes 161

15. A TIME TO HEAL 163
    Embracing the Journey 163
    Jared and Rachel's Story "There are No Coincidences" 164
    Apryl's Story "Phone Calls to Heaven!" 167

About the Author and Her Daughter 171

YEP . . . I'M A MEDIUM

Photo by Melanie Miller

Chapter 1

STEPPING INTO THE LIGHT

The Red Telephone

I remember as a kid hearing about the President of the United States having a Red Telephone. This phone was special and only used to communicate a very important message between countries. The impression this left on me was, "Wow, I would love to have a Red Telephone to connect with God!"

Here's how it went in my head: If I had a problem and needed God's help, I could just pick up the Red Telephone.

My hotline to God! I always thought just how cool would that be! I feel like I have that and much more now.

Sometimes a party line or a three-way call, and even a conference call. Oh, my goodness, I can't leave out a FaceTime session!

You might dream of winning the Lotto, but for me as an Intuitive Medium, I have won the communication with Spirit Lotto!

Yep . . . I'm a Medium, and I talk to "Spirit." It just can't get much better than that!

Introduction to Debbie P's Story

Well, life just took a U-turn and we must be on the Autobahn because there seems to be no boundaries on how fast this can go. I think any time a life change sneaks up on you like—"Oh, guess what, you are a Medium"—your breath stops, your heart skips a beat, and I'm pretty sure if I think too much about it, I might need a crash cart to defibrillate me back!

This is how I felt when I asked my friend Debbie if I could come to her house and practice on her for my first official reading. It was hard to form the words to come out of my mouth. Thank goodness I had Leo holding my entire body up as I was wilting in fear. But I did it! I took a breath and put one foot ahead of the other and trusted Leo and Spirit and officially did my first reading.

Debbie P's Story

I suppose my story begins in Cheryl's chair at her salon. Hair stylists must be trained in communication techniques and the art of allowing their clients to feel comfortable enough to share life stories. From my first appointment, I felt that comfort with Cheryl. I recall spilling details of a tragic event that took the life of a 17-year-old girl in a former community where we had lived. The girl's mother was a friend of mine and struggled so much over her loss . . . understandably so. Under advice from others, she met with a spiritual medium. Was she skeptical? Definitely! Did it help? Immensely! I won't go into detail on what she was told since this is not my story to share. Suffice it to say, the goosebumps that arose and the tears in my eyes as I relayed the story to Cheryl possibly gave her the sense that I believed. It was after this that she told me about her abilities to sense things, to read things, to feel things, even to see things. She wanted to pursue these abilities further in an effort to actually help people. Unsure of whether she'd be able to "work" under pressure, she asked if I'd be a guinea pig for her. I agreed.

Cheryl asked that before going to bed the night prior to our meeting, I think of someone I had lost. It wasn't difficult for me to decide: I missed my Aunt Ginny tremendously. She was my mom's sister and best friend. She lost her battle with cancer several years ago, but I often sensed she was around. Sometimes I'd be walking through a store and the scent of her home (coffee/cigarettes/basement) would surround me and instantly bring her to the forefront of my mind.

When Cheryl arrived at my house, nervous and with notebook in hand, she was not aware of whom I had been thinking. She actually didn't even know that I had an aunt. She told me to not give anything away—to make her "work for it," if you will. And that was my game plan. We sat on the couch together and Cheryl immediately started laughing. She said that a sassy redhead with one hand on her hip and the other holding a cup of coffee and a cigarette was quite vivid to her. Could that perhaps be the person I had been thinking of? OH YEAH! That's my Aunt Ginny. (Side note for authenticity: Nothing about me says red hair or cigarettes. I was shocked that she'd envisioned this so easily!)

She relayed to Cheryl that she was always around, watching over me, and that she thought I knew it. (That scent!)

Cheryl saw an older, very short, full-bodied woman with her, wearing a simple cotton dress and her hair set on rollers. Perfect image of my grandmother, Ginny's mom. I never saw her wear anything but a cotton dress and, by her 99th birthday, she was all of four feet eight inches tall, with a full head of hair that was regularly set on rollers! The thought of the two of them reunited was such a blessing.

When Cheryl asked me if Ginny had suffered pain with her death, I said, "Yes, but why is that important now?" She said my aunt kept dancing around, repeating, "No more pain! No more pain!" That was comforting to know, but made me question why she was still smoking cigarettes since that is what caused her cancer. Her reply to Cheryl was, "Why not?" Yes . . . Sassy still! And I love that!

A final revelation from my aunt was to tell Cheryl that she likes to attend family parties. I recall that she always loved the holidays and family reunions. She told Cheryl that she will be at our events with bells on, and that Cheryl was to put an exclamation mark on the "with bells on" part. I've yet to hear those bells ring, but have no doubt that I will.

As Cheryl's gaze shifted to my other shoulder (apparently now my dad's side), she claimed to see one of my uncles. While she was uncomfortable stating a name, this being a trial run and all, she was encouraged by "Spirit" to say the name Robert. She asked if I had lost an uncle on my dad's side named Robert. I had not. Again remember, she told me not to give anything away. She attempted to seek something/someone else but kept being pulled back to this Robert. I continued to deny having a relative named Robert who had passed. Somewhat exasperated, she pursued this path, saying that my uncle was saying the name "Robert" and it related to health issues and my mom and dad. Okay . . . that makes sense! My dad's deceased brother had a son named Robert. My cousin Robert is the owner of the ambulance service in my parents' community. When my parents have needed assistance for a serious "health issue," they call Robert first. My uncle promised to continue to guide his son in aiding my parents. More blessings.

While on my dad's side, Cheryl assured me that it wouldn't be any time soon, but that Dad's siblings were there waiting for him. When the time came for my dad to join them, it would make their family complete. They would also make sure that the transition would be easy and painless for him, and then they would have a party. She asked me if Dad was the last of the six to be living. I said he was the last, but there were only four of them. She was quite adamant that there were five siblings waiting for him. I said Dad had two brothers and a sister. Cheryl wasn't sure who the other two were . . . maybe friends, although she wasn't convinced of that. Days later in a conversation with my parents, I found out that Dad had a brother and sister who had died as infants. I never knew about them. They were the other two!

At this point in our "guinea pig" session, Cheryl and I were both feeling confident in her ability to communicate with Spirit. We were ready to wrap it up when someone named Paul (back on my mom's side) "spoke" to her. The name Paul rang no bell with me so we let it go. "Paul" was persistent though. Cheryl kept repeating, "Paul, Pauline,

Paula"... nothing. She said, "No it's just Paul... Paul Paul... PaulPaul... or Paw Paw!" Paw Paw!

Paw Paw was my grandfather, my mom's dad who passed when I was just a toddler. I only know him from pictures and stories. He relayed to Cheryl that I didn't know him, but that he had watched me grow up and he was very proud of me. And the blessings continue!

And with that, our session ended. I was left feeling so much peace and comfort. Knowing that our loved ones don't really leave us, but watch over us and protect us is so comforting. This proved to be true two years later....

My dad was admitted to the hospital, having been diagnosed with pancreatic cancer. This most painful of cancers had not been previously discovered by his doctors because Dad had never complained of any pain. By the time it was identified, it had progressed to the point where he only had a week remaining with us. The doctor had ordered morphine to be available when my dad asked for it. I had a feeling that his siblings were being true to their word in keeping Dad's pain at bay. When I told the doctor that I didn't think Dad would need the morphine, he kindly let me know how very painful this cancer is. He didn't want his patient to have to experience that. He was so surprised that Dad had gone this long without ever complaining about it. I smiled through my tears and assured him that there'd be no pain. He put his arm around me, saying it would be on order... just in case. As expected, Dad continued to deny having any pain and never requested the morphine.

At one point in his final days, he started chuckling. He mentioned seeing his best buddy (who had passed a couple of years prior). My brother and I asked if he saw anyone else. Of course, he could see his siblings. He said it looked like they were having a party! But he said there were others there, too: his three siblings and two other people. We reminded him of his brother and sister who died as infants. Dad's response was, "Oh sure! I guess that could be them. I wouldn't know what they looked like!" With his final breath, we had no doubt that they were there as promised to take care of their baby brother.

While my family's loss was tremendous and difficult, we were so extremely comforted in the words from just one brief session. I cannot thank Cheryl enough for that.

—Debbie P

Cheryl's Reflections . . .

I was so nervous to ask Debbie if I could do my first "trial run reading" with her. As I arrived at her house, thank goodness I had a sidekick: Leo! As I did her reading, he just kicked back with his ankles crossed and his hands laced behind his head. Debbie has a cathedral ceiling, so it was fun for me to watch him floating above us. He was confident and patient with me.

I will never forget her dad's siblings gathered to prepare to celebrate his arrival at a chrome kitchen table, preparing for a party. They all blessed me as much as they did Debbie with the precise detail they delivered in their messages. I will be forever grateful for Debbie and her heavenly family for breaking me in. LOL, Debbie reminded me to be sure and take Leo with me as I left!

The Screwdriver

After Debbie's dad passed, I sent her a text in regard to his services. At the last minute, I got my schedule rearranged and decided to go to the visitation. The church was about one hour and fifteen minutes from my house. I had to get ready in a flash because I was pushing it to get there before it was over. I called my husband Ben and he said be sure to drive the blacktop and highway. Needless to say, I was late enough that I took the gravel road, which was the shorter route. As I was quickly driving, I ran into a stretch of road where they had trimmed trees. All of a sudden, it sounded like I ran over a branch. I could hear it thump at each rotation of the tire.

I kept driving and, all of a sudden, the noise stopped. I was grateful thinking the branch had released its grip on me. I made it from my home to Jacksonville in about 35 minutes, and I looked down as my low tire light came on. I pulled over, got out quickly and checked my tires, and they looked okay. I hopped back in and decided to finish the drive to the church in Virginia for the visitation. My tire pressure was slowly dropping. Finally, I made it to the church and the tire was a bit low so I thought I was going to come out and it would be flat. I didn't have time for a flat tire. As soon as the visitation was over, I had to hurry back to my salon to cut my nephew's hair for his wedding.

There was a large crowd at the church. I got in line and visited with one of Debbie's friends. I made it to Debbie and her family and paid my respects. After I left, I went out to my SUV and, low and behold, the tire was still up. I drove to a local station, but he couldn't fix it so he put the spare on. You know, one of those small, weird donuts. I headed back to Jacksonville so I could cut my nephew's hair—again, a time crunch. As I was driving, the low-pressure light came on again. I called my husband and he said I better pull over. I pulled into the grade school parking lot north of town, called the local tire shop, and they came and got my vehicle. In the meantime, my daughter Lacey gave me a ride to my salon. After I cut my nephew's hair, I got a ride to the tire shop. I was afraid I had ruined my new tire. When I got there, she said they were able to fix the tire. I was so happy about that. She proceeded to say, "You won't believe what was in your tire!" She handed me a 4-inch piece of a screwdriver.

Some time passed before I told Debbie this story. When I did, she said, "That was my dad! He collected screwdrivers."

Like I have said, sometimes messages come in the strangest, coolest ways. Debbie's dad was making sure she knew that he was around!

Cheryl S. Kearns (Photo by Melanie Miller)

Chapter 2

MY LIFE

About Me

I made my entry into this world on August 10, 1961, during a rain storm. Dad mopped the rain out of the hallways of the hospital while Mom gave birth to me. I am the middle child of five kids. I always felt like I was lost or never really seen. I didn't feel like I quite fit in. I always felt a little different. True middle child stuff.

I was raised in the country outside of Pearl, Illinois. We rode and showed horses and did all of the normal things country kids do.

We always had a garden and our Pampa would bring us veggies, too. He took us fishing and frog gigging, and we would pick blackberries and strawberries with him. As kids, we climbed hills and sycamore trees, and swung on grapevines. We would swim in the creek and skate on the ponds, jump out of the hay lofts, and ride bikes just like every other kid in the country.

All of us kids loved sports. I have two sisters and two brothers so we were always busy with that. I always tried hard and did pretty well. I was never the best, but I think I worked the hardest. Softball, track, basketball, and cheerleading were my sports. I went to Pearl Grade School and East Pike High School in Milton (about eight miles north of Pearl). That is where I met my husband Ben. He was a senior and I was a sophomore when his friends got us together. He has always been my "Knight in Shining Armor" and still is! He has put up with my ups and downs, supported me, and stayed by my side even when I didn't deserve it. God sent me Ben, for this I am certain and completely grateful! We celebrated 39 years of marriage in September, 2018.

I got out of high school a year early to go to cosmetology school. I was on the fast track to move life forward. I stayed enrolled in high school, completed a correspondence course to get my last one-half credit, and graduated with my class in 1979.

I attended Flamingo Beauty College in Jacksonville, Illinois and rented an apartment there. I worked at Leo's Pizza delivering pizzas that year. I graduated in March, had hernia surgery in June and, while I was in the hospital, I received my letter that I had passed my cosmetology boards! Then Ben and I married September 15, 1979. That was a busy year!

Ben was a farmer with his family at the time and still farms today. After five years of marriage we had our daughter and four years later our son. They have both married and I am blessed with seven wonderful grandkids.

I worked as a hairstylist in Pittsfield for 18 months and then I joined Ben's aunt in Milton. We later bought that shop and worked together for 25 years. I took my first yoga class in 2002, saw a holistic healer, cleaned up my diet, and started working on the emotional healing aspect that started the ball rolling.

In 2006, Ben and I bought renovated an old building in downtown Jacksonville and opened Inner Harmony Day Spa and Salon. We continue to offer complete hair services in addition to nails, facials, massage, yoga, karate, and now, intuitive readings. It's been a journey of growth, lessons, opportunity, and change.

The rest I will share in the chapters to come. I had no idea all of this would lead me to becoming a Medium!

My Childhood Memories

What do you remember as a kid? Most Psychics and Mediums have these amazing stories. They talk about seeing and talking to Ghosts or Spirits from a young age. That's not really the case for me.

As a young child, I was kind of shy. To know me now, you would say . . . NOT! I say I didn't see or talk to Spirits, but now I know that I could feel them there. I can remember going outside at night to feed the dogs and running back to the house in a panic, knowing that someone was behind me. Funny thing, now that I realize Spirits really were behind me.

The only place in the house that I ever felt safe was under the bed with my back to the wall, where nothing was behind me.

We all feel energy. I just didn't know what I was feeling as a kid. When I would walk into a room, I could feel—and I thought almost hear—what they were thinking about me. I knew if they wanted me there or not. I just never gave this any thought. I just thought everyone felt like me. What I wasn't aware of is I really was hearing their thoughts and feelings. My friend Raymon Grace, who is a great dowser, puts it like this: Go to a house to a birthday party and feel the energy and go to the funeral home and feel the energy. We can all feel that, and that is just the tip of the iceberg on tuning into and sensing Spirit.

I have always felt like the black sheep of the family, never completely fitting in. I often wonder why I chose this journey. I remember a couple of stories that were told to me about my childhood. Once they were looking for me and couldn't find me. Finally, they found me behind the barn where fence posts were leaned against the back of the barn. I had crawled back in there and gone to sleep. They thought I had been bitten by a rattlesnake and was dead. That was a fair thought because we lived about one mile from Rattlesnake Den, which was very appropriately named.

In another story, our family was swimming at the creek and, all of a sudden, they couldn't find me. Then they saw bubbles and the top of my head. I had walked straight out into the water. They jumped in and pulled me out.

Now I look back on these memories and stories and realize I have a purpose to fulfill in this lifetime. It just wasn't my time to die quite yet.

Yep, I guess I am a square peg in a round hole in our family, but truth is I had life lessons to experience and rise above.

Have you ever had a reoccurring dream that made you almost not want to go to sleep because you knew it was coming? That was me! I feel like I had this dream a thousand times.

In the dream, I was always in our bedroom. There are five kids in our family, so we shared a bedroom, four of us at this time. This bedroom was small. It was narrow and long. On each end was a clothes bar with a shelf above it. They were closets with no doors. The room's doorway was in the middle of the wall and the outside wall had two windows. In the dream, the room would be on fire and filled with smoke. A tiger was coming in the door and I was on the left in the closet with no door, hiding behind a beach bag. This dream was exactly the same each time I dreamed it. It was in great detail. I could see the colors of the blue and yellow on the front of the beach bag and feel the heat and smell the smoke.

I was afraid and trying to figure out how I was going to get out alive. If I tried to run to get out the door, the tiger would devour me. If I stayed, the fire or smoke would kill me. So I had no way out! I would crouch down behind that beach bag, knowing it couldn't save me, and then I would wake up. Again and again as a child and then as an adult, I would have this dream or nightmare, over and over.

I finally quit having this dream once it was explained to me by a Reiki Master in 2002. He simply said the fire is your emotions, the smoke is your feelings. Now, who is the tiger and who is the beach bag? I experienced a life-altering child trauma so the tiger was my abuser and the beach bag was the person I wanted to save me but couldn't. I was a changed person after that and I never had the dream again.

I had to tell you this story because it is a part of what makes me who I am. But how we grow or not is how we advance our Souls. I choose to grow and be stronger and better so I can help others.

The Truth Will Set You FREE, you know!

You can't force life. So much in our childhood is a direct channeling from Spirit and for some reason, some of us just don't recognize it.

Most of us don't realize that all of the things we do in life growing up are preparing us for our Life Purpose. You know, the real reason you came to earth. Now, you just have to uncover it. My advice to you is never give up the search for what your "True Life Purpose" is! It's worth not giving up on!

What is Your Life Purpose?

As my friend Cathy always says, "I wish I knew my Life Purpose!" That's the million-dollar question! I was in search of or trying to find mine all of my life. I just didn't know it. As a child I always knew I was supposed to help people.

When you are a child, or should I say when I was a child, I didn't know I was searching for an answer. I just knew that I was going to help people. My family called me "little buttinsky." I was always butting in. I just wanted to be seen! I would stand in church as we were singing hymns and would hear in my head, "You need to help people." As I sat there and listened to the scary hellfire and damnation sermons, I would talk to God in my heart and I would say, "My God is love, my God is love, my God is love," over and over. And he would say, "You are going to help people!"

You know as a young child, it seemed so simple. Then you start to grow up and life gets a little less simple. You go through the regular struggles of growing, but the part I didn't know was that I really was talking to God and not only was He listening—He was talking back.

Okay, God, so how am I going to help people? When I was about 11 years old, I visited my cousins' house in the summer and we often went to the public pool. I was always uncomfortable. One, I hated swimsuits and two, I couldn't really swim that well. I learned to swim in our creek so I felt out of place with the city kids who could swim like fish. I knew they probably took lessons and they did this every day.

So here we go, me feeling like a duck out of water and I could feel everyone looking at me. I stood out like a sore thumb! But, okay, here we go!

In the middle of this pool was a big concrete square, like an island. You could swim out there and play off of it, so my cousins and I headed out. All I could think of was that I couldn't wait until we were done. These kids could swim and I felt so inadequate. I was heading to the island and I was walking through the water. There were tons of kids and it was so loud and chaotic. I saw a small blonde boy struggling to get to the island. He was swimming, but he wasn't quite tall enough to reach the bottom to touch where he could keep his head above water. He went under as he tried to swim out to it. As he struggled to swim, he went under a second time. The lifeguards didn't see him and then he went under a third time. I made it to him and grabbed him and helped him to the concrete island! He was grateful and I was able to help. Mission accomplished: I helped someone. For that short time, I felt like I was doing what I was supposed to be doing in life—helping people. That same day, there was a girl who was in trouble in the same scenario and I helped her, too. I remember being thankful that I saw them. The lifeguards didn't have a chance to see them because the kids in the pool were so thick you could have stirred them with a stick. It felt good to be able to help someone!

We all have stories like this. They sure seem pretty generic when I think about it, but this was one of my life lessons and "ah-ha" moments. It felt as right as rain for me to help someone.

You Can't Force Life

I never felt like I belonged in my family. One time my older brother told me, "Look, you must be adopted because we all have brown hair and you have blonde" (normal sibling stuff). It is hard as a child to not feel wanted or accepted, but I'm sure most of us have felt that, or maybe not. If not, count your lucky stars.

What I have found in life is you just can't force it. I guess you can, but it never produces happiness. Happiness comes when you get into the ebb and flow of life. You dance with the rhythm of life. When we go against the grain, we struggle.

I never realized I was rowing against the current until I embraced true life—the life I was meant to live. Now keep in mind, this goes against family values, social values, and small town mindedness, but yes, I did it. I jumped in head first!

It is a comfort now, though, to know why I could feel their stuff when I walked into a room. It all makes sense now that I'm an Intuitive Medium.

Some of my fondest memories as a child were with my younger brother who was born on my second birthday. We shared so much as kids and I know Spirit sent him to help me through all of those tough times. He was the one person who never judged me; he just accepted and understood who I really am. I'm not sure if I would have made it without him! To this day I am grateful he accepted the mission to be my brother and my childhood best friend. Spirit always has a plan!

Ten Talents

I remember as a child the parable of the talents. This story in the Bible always worried me. I can remember thinking about it and trying to understand it. This was my understanding of it: The master was leaving and gave one man five talents, one man two talents, and one man one talent. These talents were valued coins. The first man invested his and so did the second man, each of them doubling their talents. The third man buried his out of fear of losing it. When the master returned, he was very happy with the first two servants who invested and doubled the amount. He was very disappointed with the servant he gave one talent, who only returned with it out of fear that he would lose it. I can remember thinking that I would not be the servant who buried his talent out of fear. To me, this parable meant if God gives you an ability, you better use it to grow what he has given you.

So, fast forward to July, 2013 when Leo passed and came through with messages to my daughter Lacey and me. First, how do you ignore such a calling? Yes, fear stepped in to say, "But you own a business, and family and friends and people and the church will shun you." Of course, we deal with all of that and, yes, that all came true—but bottom line is God gave us these "talents," and I won't bury mine. It is NOT an option for me! So as it goes, I will keep doing readings and delivering healing messages because He gave me the "talent," and I will increase it. What a disappointment it would be for me, when I cross over, to set at the feet of God and feel his disappointment. He gave me the tools. I want to hear, "Well done my good and faithful servant." So I will soldier on and listen to Spirit, not man.

Answering the Call

When does that moment come when you think, "This is what all the other things that I have done in life has led me to?" My Life Purpose!

I think we all, or well, most of us (or should I say, some of us), come into life with the question: "What is My Life Purpose?"

Sometimes we focus so much on the question that we don't see what is right in front of us. You know that old saying, "You can't see the forest for the trees."

I have always known that I am here to help people. I just didn't know how I was to do it. When I reflect on my life, I realize it wasn't just one thing, it was many. Each has led to the other and now here I am, an Intuitive Medium helping Spirit deliver healing messages to their loved ones still here on earth.

Moving Away from Negative People

Light attracts light. We have all heard that, but do we really realize how true that statement is? I can tell you this is very powerful. I can also tell you light also attracts dark.

As a business owner, I have witnessed and felt this truth. When you have positive employees who are honest and trustworthy, it shows. When you have that one person whom you think you can fix, the boat will get rocked. They seem to be able to plant negative doubts in the whole crew. Your best plan of action is to throw the negative person overboard, as harsh as that sounds. Once you purge the negative out of your life and the dust settles, the positive is then released for the healing.

When I started a three-year path to become a yoga teacher, I learned many hard lessons. My concept was anyone who was teaching had to be honest and above reproach. I was wrong. It broke my heart to learn the truth. I am a die-hard believer in giving a person a second chance, but don't fool yourself. As my friend Raymon told me, "You can't fix everyone because everyone doesn't want to be fixed." Some people don't realize they are broken or even dark. My Achilles heel is I think I can change people. I always want to believe they want to be honest, trustworthy, and kind. Sadly, that is not always the case. Be careful who you choose to help and always protect yourself.

I had the belief system that everyone is striving to be better. I now choose my friends wisely. Do I miss or have a glimpse of hope that there is good in everyone? Yes, I do, and I guess that means I still have hard lessons to learn, but hopefully they won't be as painful, as my eyes are wide open.

As a Medium, I have insight on what's coming. I try my best to stay out of the way. We all need to learn our lessons. I just step back and watch it unfold.

The Spirit World allows us a view of what's to come and even when we see their darkness, we just have to wait and watch. What is interesting is they don't want to see their own darkness, due to the ego. As we hold the light, sometimes that is all we can do!

Letting Go

To get to where I am now on my journey in life, I had a lot to heal first. I was fortunate to find a holistic healer who I saw monthly for 11 years. She did wonderful body work on me and opened the door to so many healing modalities! She introduced me to dowsing, card readings, Soul channeling, energy balancing, and much more.

She became my teacher and mentor. I called her a friend, but in all reality, I was her client. She taught me so much through the years. She would push me and I would come back for more. Sometimes to grow, we have to leave behind that which we so rely on!

Spirit has a way of revealing things to us at just the perfect time! I put her on a pedestal, that's for sure. But Spirit had a bigger picture for me. If I had stayed under her, I never would have grown and stepped out to be an Intuitive Medium!

She told me once that "I knew things," but I had no idea what that meant. Hind sight is 20/20 and now I can see it all clearly.

Lacey and I were taking mentoring classes under her. She demanded a lot from us and at times seemed harsh with her teaching approach. At the last session with her in March, 2013, she kept pushing me until, as I see it, Spirit showed me her true self.

We were in the basement room of a building where she rented space. It was on a Sunday and the owner showed up unexpectedly to show the spaces to some prospective renters. My mentor was taken by surprise. She hadn't let the owner know that she was using the space and hadn't paid her rent for that day!

For anyone who knows me, I am very honest and cannot stand dishonesty. She proceeded with our training that day and continued to push me. I was struggling on how to articulate my words the way she wanted me to during our training. Thankfully, Lacey helped me form the question for the session in a way my mentor wanted. Needless to say, I was beyond frustrated.

I always tried my best to please her and make her proud of me. When we started these mentoring classes, she asked each of us what we wanted out of the training. My answer was to get closer to Spirit! Much to my surprise, the next statement that came out of her mouth that day crushed me. She told me "I was disconnected from God!" You might as well have buried me on the spot! I cried for days over this. "I have failed God," I thought.

Once I got over my pity party—thanks to my daughter Lacey, my husband Ben, and my best friend Cathy—I got up and brushed myself off. I was done (thanks to Spirit) with the mentorship! I was to move forward on my path. Without these two extreme lessons I think I would still be in her shadow and not fulfilling my true Life Purpose.

The thing in life that I have always known, and Spirit knew this, is I have always been strongly connected to God. Mic Drop!

Photo by Lacey Matthews

Chapter 3

EVER CHANGING

Something Unpredictable

When you look into a child's eyes, you see hope, possibilities, joy, adventure, and endless stories to be written. That's what I saw when I looked into Leo's eyes: a young man full of love, kindness, charm, and life being lived to the fullest.

Then that terrible phone call came on July 18, 2013. Leo Alfano and his girlfriend Morgan McKinnon died in a tragic motorcycle accident. Leo and Morgan were working at his parents' pizza place. You know kids and their young love. They couldn't wait to get off work to be together. Leo's brother Peter let them off early that evening. Leo had borrowed his dad's motorcycle that evening because the week before he had his pickup truck in the county fair truck pull. The tailgate got damaged and his tail lights weren't working. Leo didn't want to get a ticket so he parked the truck and rode the motorcycle to work. They left work, hopped on the motorcycle, and headed south through town toward Leo's parents' house. As they rode through South Jacksonville, they were coming up to the intersection at Comfort Drive. The light was green so they headed through it. There was an SUV heading north through the intersection that didn't see Leo and Morgan on the motorcycle and turned left directly in front of them, causing the fatal accident.

NO, NO! It can't be! My dear friends just lost their son!! How does a person wrap their head around that devastation, that life-altering moment? I will never forget the impact this news had on the whole community! Could someone please press the rewind button?! Can we just go back in time to make a small adjustment to avoid this life-altering moment? Out of this horrible accident, this heart-stopping moment, came the unraveling of my story as a Medium!

Back in 1978, Leo's family moved here from Italy and opened Leo's Pizza in downtown Jacksonville, Illinois. When I was 17 years old, I worked for them, delivering pizzas after I got out of class. They had just opened that year and right next door to the pizza place, I was attending Flamingo Beauty College to become a hair stylist. Leo's grandparents opened the pizza place and raised their three young children there.

I don't believe in coincidence, but who would know that after 27 years I would open Inner Harmony Day Spa and Salon across the street from them and their daughter Tonia and I would become close friends.

Tonia is married to Sam and they had three kids: Peter, Filie, and Leo. They were all raised at the pizza place, too.

When I opened my salon, Tonia would come over for haircuts and Leo soon followed on his own. I loved when he would walk in my door after he strolled across the street from the pizza place and say, "Hey, Cheryl." I'd reply, "Do you need a haircut, Leo?" He would give me that smile that I couldn't resist and say, "Yeah." I always found time to work him in. Leo had charm about him that I couldn't resist. His boyish charm, topped off with his Italian charm, got me every time.

Who knew at 17, I would meet a family that, some 30 years later, would impact my life path drastically. We go through our daily duties in life and don't even realize it's all important. I have been on a Spiritual Search for the past 16 plus years. I have grown tremendously during that time, but I'm not sure if I would have ever made this leap of faith if it weren't for Leo. It's like being slapped in the face or having cold water thrown on you: it gets your attention immediately. He gave me courage to step forward and begin to fulfill my Life Purpose. I have known for a long time the direction I needed to go and have been working with amazing mentors. Maybe it's a timing thing, but I really know in my heart it was Leo who gave me the courage to step out of the shadows and really make a difference while I am here.

When youth halts and moments stop and the rest of the chapters seem like blank pages, how do you go on? This is the burning question! I stopped to finally buy a card for the family and as I looked through them, I thought, "How do you put into words the very thing you hope never passes over your lips?" Words are never enough and time is too short. Can't we just hit that rewind button? We try as we may, but it all seems so trivial in the scheme of things. As I sit to write in the card, nothing comes. I want it to flow out of me like a river of comfort to the family I love and that is hurting so deeply, but again, nothing. Well, nothing that seems to matter. So finally I settle for a few (as I see it) empty words. Not empty on feelings, just no poetic magic. That's it: the magic wand. Why didn't I think of that? Wave the wand and everything goes back as it was before "The Great Sadness!" There is nothing great about sadness, that's for sure.

How do you measure when you should be there and when you should give them their private time? I tried to listen to Spirit on this one. I have found that when you sit quietly and go with your gut (intuition, if you will), that's what is usually best.

I talked to Tonia several times that day and wanted to go be with them, but I chose to wait and go the next day. I think I listened to logic instead of Spirit. I asked her about coming and she wanted to see what Sam wanted to do that day. I had a feeling it was going to be a hard day for them—and it was.

Sam and Tonia both told me that it was a really hard day. It was a very heavy and sad day for them. So did I listen to Spirit and was it best that they were alone to have a sad day, or should I have been there? The next day I didn't call because my gut said . . . get out there. I arrived to find Sam and his brother sitting outside. You could have cut the sadness with a knife. Why are the words never there when you need them most? We hugged and talked for a couple of minutes, then he told me that Tonia was inside. I went in to find her and saw Filie. We couldn't find Tonia inside or out. Sam said, "I know she went in." She was out on the deck talking on the phone with a friend from Italy. There has been a universal outpouring of love for this family. They have their American friends and family and their Italian friends and family. It takes a universe, you know, to get through something like this.

I don't know if every Italian family is like this, but every time you show up at their house, they have to feed you. They were just putting the pasta on the table and even though I had just eaten a salad—nothing doing—I had to eat some pasta. Her dad had made the sauce and it was wonderful. I'm glad they forced this meal on me! I gave the card to them and told them to open it later, so Tonia tucked it away. After lunch we talked for a couple of hours.

I had to leave and check on work at Inner Harmony. When I was at work, all I could think about was Sam and Tonia. The kids, Sam, and her dad had left for Peter's pizza place in Pittsfield. Sam's brother also had to leave. I asked Tonia if she wanted to go with me, but she said she had cards to go through and other stuff to do. When you can't get someone off your mind, you should do something about it. I got to my business about 15 minutes or so away and as soon as I walked in, I told Lacey I hated to leave Tonia. I knew they needed time alone, but I felt like I should go back. Lacey said she would like to go see her so we decided after work in a couple of hours we would see if Malik (Lacey's son) wanted to go with us and drive back out. That's what we did and I am grateful Leo kept pushing us to do so. It was a good night.

On the Friday after Leo passed, we were at Sam and Tonia's house and you could feel Leo everywhere. Lacey, her husband Jelani, and their three kids (Malik who was nine, Nevaeh, five, and Kenyon, three) all went to their home with me. Leo has brought many messages through Malik. At the time, Malik could see Spirit in 3D (like we see people), complete form, as if they were still in their bodies. He was a great catalyst that sad night.

We were hoping for Leo to be a chatter box that night. This was the first time we have taken Malik to be the Medium between Spirits and people. I think Leo knew Malik was a little overwhelmed because they were both quiet. Nine is awfully young to be taking him out on the road, so to speak! Malik told Sam that Leo was standing right beside him, which brought great comfort to Sam.

There is this sad heaviness that hangs over his family and loved ones which seems can't be lifted or even pierced to allow any happiness back into their lives. Who can be happy or even move forward from this point? Leo is doing his best to change all of that. He is working to somehow bring some peace and happiness back to those he loved and touched so deeply while he was here. How do you move on with all the sadness just looming over you? I know that is the state my friends are in. It's like being stuck in quicksand and no one can reach you to save you. You are helpless, crying out, broken-hearted and, as Tonia put it, you just want to wrap yourself in a cocoon and never emerge again. Stuck in the pain, lifeless, done, how can you go on? It's not fair to ever think you should feel joy or happiness again. That's where you are after such sorrow has swept in and destroyed your life as you knew it.

Do you wake up each morning and wonder why you are here? If so, if every day is, "Who am I," "What am I supposed to do in my life," you probably aren't living your Life Purpose. That's how it has been for me, until now. Leo changed all of that. How is it that one event in life can open your eyes to your true Life Purpose? Here I am, a hair stylist, yoga teacher, business owner, and now, REALLY . . . a Medium? Who knew in a blink of an eye, in one moment in time, that life could change so completely. We hear it happening all around us, but really, do we ever think it will be us? An event, a tragedy, a moment in time and it's done. Changed! Who are you now? My story is probably very different from yours or anyone else's whom Leo was connected to.

I think Leo is on his "Spirit Life Mission!" This is what has brought me to this point in time in my life. Now I clearly see my Life Purpose! When I was little girl, I always knew that I was sent here to help people. Thanks, Leo, for the fact that you won't let me stay behind the scenes anymore. You have now placed me on the front line of this battle that I have struggled with for so many years.

I have heard many stories of Leo, from many different walks of life. You might say he was diversified and great at life. We all won't get to be talked about so warmly and leave the imprint that Leo left with us. I challenge each of you to take a step in the right direction and be, as one friend said, more "Leo-like." When I heard her say that it really made my heart smile and for his family to hear this, it had to have been one of the proudest moments. Leo was multifaceted, to say the least, and if you had the pleasure to meet him, I think you were touched by a special Soul!

Losing Leo changed life forever for so many—including myself—but for me it goes beyond the normal loss of emotions that affect us. For me and Lacey, it has changed our lives on a much different level. Because of Leo, we now are Intuitive Mediums, or Psychic Mediums as it's more commonly called. Yes, we talk to and deliver messages from those Souls that have crossed over to the Other Side. We never know why things happen and how it will change our life path.

I know this concept is hard for a lot of people to accept, as it was for us in the beginning. Let me tell you our story and you can decide for yourself.

I think when we were in Spirit form on the Other Side, we sat down with God and he showed us several scenarios (families, if you will) and we looked at all of them and said, "I choose this one." Now, for what reason I'm not sure, but I am sure it had to do with growth, life lessons, and how we help each other. Have you ever met someone and felt like you have known them all your life? Or had a déjà vu moment. I think we all have done this, many times. Life that is!

I remember three past lives that I have had. You might not agree in past lives. I didn't used to either, but things change us in life, and then another facet is revealed to us and we see another piece of the puzzle. At first, it might not seem to fit into our cookie-cutter mind, but then it feels as right as rain! You know the one that was drilled into you with all good intention, but it shaded your mind. It kept us in a box of this is how life is and has to be! The dogma has been set!

You guessed it! I stepped out of the box and there is a whole new world out there and it's fabulous! Here is the sadness to my, as some would say, Awakening. It took my dear friends losing a son at 19 years old to jolt me into seeing my Life Purpose.

Like you, I have many childhood memories—some good and some not so good. Really, is that fair to say or is it some memories to grow on? We learn from every experience we have in life. It's what you do with it that counts. You know the old saying, "What doesn't kill you makes you stronger." I became a fighter! Knock me down if you so choose, but I will be sure to get back up and, you got it, stand even stronger!

Do we have scars? Probably, but those, too, can be beneficial on our path. I don't know about you, but I'm pretty sure I didn't ask for a free ride. Look at your life! I mean really look at it! Those bumps in the road are just that—bumps. Some literally suck the life right out of you!

Death. What is it really? That will always be a mystery! What we know is that it is certain like a sunset and sunrise, it's coming, but until we experience it, it is unknown. Leo and the Spirit World are our catalysts to this unknown territory. Each time we hear from Spirit, it makes it a little less scary, even more exciting, if you will. Now as my journey has made a huge shift, I could finally make it to this point. Lacey and I do readings for those who have lost loved ones. We do it so they can find peace and know that their loved ones are safe, happy, and still with them. So stay tuned so I can share my journey with Lacey as Inner Harmony Mediums, and many readings from others who this process has helped bring healing and comfort on their life journey. It's been a crazy ride so far and I am sure that it is to be continued!

So, You're a Witch?

Since Leo told me to write this book, I have been afraid that I wouldn't have enough material to fill it. Now I see all I have to do is keep doing this work and the book will write itself.

Lacey and her husband were house hunting. Three kids in a two-bedroom house seems to lead you down that path. They found a house that they might be interested in and asked me to come look and see what I thought about it. As we rounded the last corner of the house, their realtor mentioned he heard we did medium work at my business. I replied, "Yes, we do." He asked how we got into that and I replied, "When God talks, you listen." He stopped me right after I said God and said, "Oh, that's not from God!" He further explained that the Old Testament tells us not to do that. I quickly explained that the New Testament doesn't speak of it and I was taught it overrides the Old. He replied, "So, you just ignore the Old Testament?"

Now keep in mind I am only speaking from what I was taught in the years in the church. I explained to him that each denomination of church is different and we all have the right to believe differently. In other words, you have your belief system and I have mine. Keep in mind that I used to be exactly like this man. I wouldn't let my kids read their horoscopes or watch shows on TV that I thought were going against my church. In my childhood church, you couldn't even have music in it because you were only to make music in your heart, according to our doctrine. After I married my husband, we started to attend his family's church and they accompanied the hymn service with a piano. It took me a long time to embrace the fact that the musical instrument in the service wasn't going to send me to hell. As human beings, we all do our best to read and translate the doctrine of the Church to the best of our ability and to what our religion teaches us. I think the old adage of "To each their own" applies here. The next thing the realtor asked as he chuckled was, "So, are you a witch?" I quickly replied "No," but what I was hearing from my helpers from the Other Side was, "Well, not in this lifetime!" I knew that was adding fuel to the fire so I chose to keep that to myself. He then asked who was doing the readings and I told him my daughter Lacey and myself. I thought the conversation was over, but thanks to Leo, I had one more thing to add. I asked this man, "What if Leo were standing right in front of you (in Spirit form) and wanted you to help his family? Could you turn him down? I could not!" I'm sure this will not be the last of this type of judgment, but I work for God and I am pretty sure he asks us to leave the judging to him. So Be It!

You must understand that this is the very reason that I have been "hiding under a bush," as the Vacation Bible School song goes. All I have ever wanted to do is do what is right in God's eyes. I don't want people to judge me, but that is inevitable. People judge every day. I see that God hands us a talent and says go and see what you can do with it. I will not be the one who returns with that same talent and not multiply it as he wished. When given a talent and hiding it under a bush, you don't grow, nor do you do anyone a favor by keeping it to yourself. Where would we be as a whole if everyone hid their talents? I am grateful every day that we have people who were courageous, stepped out and put their fear to the side, and made a difference so we can all grow and become better human beings!

I have struggled for years on this very thing and now I have stepped out of the fear to help others heal by helping them connect to their loved ones on the Other Side!

This might be a small contribution to mankind, but it is the way that I know I can help and so I will push on! I have heard people's cries for years and always wished I could help or say something that could help them heal, even if it were only a little. Maybe I am just a drop in the ocean, but aren't we all? Together we are the ocean—so do your part, step out of your fear, and do what you can do to help heal mankind!

Deb D's Story

When I first saw a couple of Mediums on TV, my first impression was there is no way they can do that! People are telling them the things, but boy, the first time after losing our son I went to Lacey for a massage and she was telling me things there was no way she knew, asking me about the chocolate ice cream cone. My son and I would always go to this little ice cream place. Then I, our daughter, and grandson had a private group session with Lacey and Cheryl. At first, they made us feel really good knowing Travis was okay. They talked about the car he got the grandson, about the word "sunshine"—boy, that was a saying of his, "Good Morning Sunshine." There was other stuff that was personal. Then our next session we had in December, 2017, knowing that he told them that I was keeping things bottled up, so how right they were. You cannot hide anything from these two. So now I have changed my mind about Mediums. They know everything and can tell you a lot to help you get through these difficult times. They care about everyone and make you feel like family. Thanks Cheryl and Lacey for what you do.

—Deb D

Lacey's Reflections . . .

I don't remember the first time Deb came to me as a massage client, but I remember one massage in great detail. I don't like to intertwine being a Medium and Massage Therapist unless I know they are open to both.

I didn't know Deb well enough yet as a client and when her son came through during her massage, I really wasn't sure IF or even HOW I wanted to deliver his messages. I also don't remember how many times she had been in or if it was the first time she had come in for a massage. I remember doing about 45 minutes of her one-hour massage, continuing to receive messages from her son and having an internal debate with myself on how I was supposed to broach the subject of being a Medium with this client who I had yet to really get to know. Her son continued to be pretty demanding and, as hard as it was for me, I remember finally just kind of blurting it out.

I remember thinking, "What's the worst that can happen." She may not believe me and that's okay, but my heart would not be able to handle NOT delivering these messages from her son. I don't remember the exact messages he came through with, but I remember laughing at how random some of them appeared to me to be. He knew they were exactly the things his mom needed to hear to know that it was him. I have learned that regardless of how uncertain or uncomfortable we may be delivering a message, Spirit will be relentless until the message is delivered, and it is always exactly what that person needs at that moment in time.

JoAnn's Story

My friend JoAnn's son Matt took his own life on September 22, 2014, after suffering from depression for many years. When Matt comes through to JoAnn, the thing that stands out is he is always smiling!

On Christmas Day that year, she went up to check on the coolers in her flower shop. She had a van that she always left sitting in the parking lot at her business. When she arrived at the business, she pulled in next to her van. She looked over and right behind the driver's seat on the window, someone had drawn a smiley face! She knew it was Matt leaving a message for her.

I have read for JoAnn before and one of the things that I told her was to ask for something specific from Matt. Always ask in great detail.

Matt has a daughter and JoAnn knew he was taking care of her so she never asked him for anything until four years after his passing. She remembered what I told her and she asked him to come to her in her dreams. She dreamed of him that night. He was sitting in the passenger seat in that work van, exactly where he had drawn the smiley face!

The week of the four-year anniversary of his death, JoAnn woke up hearing Matt crying. This was a familiar cry as JoAnn heard it for several months after his passing. It was so hard for JoAnn to hear Matt crying! This time it was right before Christmas. She said she wanted to open her eyes, but she was afraid he would leave. As she lay there with her eyes closed listening to Matt crying, she told him "It's okay to go!" It's just like when we have a loved one who is dying and we whisper to them . . . it's okay to let go. . . . They often are waiting to hear those words from us. They then know we will be okay.

JoAnn put it beautifully: "Some people have the sense and are in tune with God, to feel their peace in their presence. It's peace for our Soul and peace for their Soul!"

In 2018 through her loss, JoAnn started a support group in honor of Matt and all of the parents who have lost a child to suicide. She calls it "Hope Lives On!" It's a healing group where people share their stories of comfort that they know their loved ones are still with them.

They support and comfort each other. They share their tears and then the families all go their separate ways. It's a safe place for healing!

JoAnn shared with me that she did this in honor of Matt. The night before the fourth anniversary of his death, I asked her, "I don't know, should I call it his anniversary?" JoAnn replied with a sense of peace about her, "It's his fourth heavenly birthday!" I love how JoAnn said this and then she spoke of seeing cardinals as a sign from Matt. She knows he's around her all the time!

Our loved ones work really hard to send us a sign of comfort and peace. The next time you see a cardinal, a butterfly, or a feather, know that it is a sign from your loved ones that they will always be with you!

Cheryl's Reflections . . .

JoAnn is a dear friend who I met when my daughter was planning her wedding. JoAnn did Lacey's flowers for her special day. It's funny how Spirit brings us together. We now have businesses side by side in Jacksonville. The many times I have read for JoAnn, many family members and friends have come through with such detail. Matt has always been a little reserved. Spirit always knows who or what we need at the precise time. It is a timing thing! The perfect message at the perfect time. Just like the smiley face right before Christmas. Holidays are especially hard for families.

We sometimes need self-healing time and JoAnn is the most unselfish, kind person I know. She wanted Matt to take care of everyone else, leaving her for last.

I am so glad she listened to Spirit as I conveyed to her about being specific. She asked her son to come and he did!

Photo by Lacey Matthews

Chapter 4

FOR THE LOVE OF LEO

Journaling

What a great way to get your thoughts and feelings out of you. I went through several years that I journaled nearly every day. It was so cleansing and healing for me. As I write this book, I have revisited my old journals and they have been helpful in so many ways.

I dated them, so as a timeline, they have been priceless. When I read them, they feel so much different now as compared to then as I wrote them. I can see and feel my Spiritual Growth that has occurred through the years. Some harder times of my life I wrote and then did a ceremonial fire and tossed them in so they could burn and rise to the Heavens for release.

All of the processes I have learned or am still learning are helpful at each level or stage of my Spiritual Growth. The gratitude I have for all of these modalities is something words can't describe.

The journaling came at a time in my life that needed a lot of healing. It was such a great way to let it out and allow that space in me to then heal. Some of my journals seem simple and juvenile at times, but that also made me realize that we are infants in Spirit that grow to, hopefully, one day mature into a well-seasoned Spiritual adult human being.

Introduction to Tonia's Story

I wish I weren't writing this part of my story. I wish Leo was playing a different role in my life as opposed to being my Spirit Guide. The loss of a child is a parent's greatest pain! Leo's journey on earth was a short 19 years, but his mark on all of us is enormous! I wish you could see what I see and you would understand why he had to cross over. Leo is a very special Soul! Here we might call him the Golden Child. He was the favorite child (as he so often put it)! So I am going to tell you he is the Golden Soul! He is a few levels higher on the Other Side. He has a bigger job to do. The work he does now is of the utmost importance. Fly high Leo and keep doing what you were born to do. Just be you because you are something special!

Tonia's Story

I know that these deaths were meant to be on this day July 18, 2013. Leo Alfano and Morgan McKinnon and the many events that led up to that moment show us it was God's will and their time. Leo's truck's rear lights were getting fixed so he took the Harley, and we switched days with Suzie to work at Leo's Pizza. Morgan worked that night to pick up extra money to go to Italy. Peter, like usual, let Leo go home half an hour earlier so he could be with Morgan a little longer.

I don't know how we will go on, but I know that it is with God's Grace giving us strength, and I don't underestimate the power of the thousands of people praying that we will stay strong. I feel that I have taken the power of prayer for granted. I miss my Leo. My heart aches for him and for my husband. I find myself asking Leo to ask God to intervene and help him more than me to get through it!

The next day after the accident, my brother's girlfriend and I were scrolling through her phone photos so I could get a picture of Leo and Morgan together. I thought to myself, "I wish that I could get that picture that we found on her phone in a poster size, framed." The next day, these three kids showed up at my house with that picture we saw on the phone, full poster size, framed! They had no idea that we had looked at the exact picture earlier. Leo is in full swing delivering signs already.

Morgan and Leo were at it again. Morgan's parents had picked out her casket and we had no idea which one they picked. When we picked out Leo's, Sam was drawn to the one that had black with chrome all over it. Sam said he felt Leo saying, "Don't let Mom bury me in an old man's casket!" We ended up picking the same one as Morgan's parents picked except hers was blue and Leo's was black. We feel that Leo and Morgan actually led us to them.

A few days after the services, Sam was planting a tree in Leo's memory and as soon as he was done, Leo's favorite song came on the radio. I know that Leo was acknowledging his father.

One day we were sitting at our kitchen table talking and heard bell-like sounds coming from the hallway by the bathroom, next to Leo's bedroom. Then minutes after that, the front screen door opened and shut. We thought it was my husband Sam, but realized soon after that it was our Leo! Soon after while looking for my phone, I opened the desk drawer because I heard music coming out of my iPod. I put the earplugs in my ears and the song "Don't Worry Child" by Swedish Mafia was playing. I started crying and thanked Leo for the beautiful gift.

Leo and Morgan's candlelight vigil was July 29 at 9 p.m. Over one thousand people were there, including the Jacksonville High School Band Drum Line. Before the drum line started, Filie, Peter, and a friend had Leo's truck in the soccer field with 98 motorcycles following them like a parade to get things started. These kids only planned that two hours prior to the start of the candlelight vigil. That shows you how much this tragedy affected people. You only had to mention Leo and Morgan, and people would do anything to honor them. When my husband Sam and I arrived, we were walking onto the soccer field and Sam smiled and turned to me with such honor and said, "Who was this kid?" His soccer coach talked about Leo and Morgan and their families. Then we watched the DVD made of Leo and Morgan on a big screen, all seated on the soccer field at dusk. We all lit candles and the lanterns and then released them. As we looked up at the sky, the clouds formed a picture of Leo and Morgan looking down at us. Unbelievable! Another Sign!

One of Leo's friends called and told me she was looking through a drawer while cleaning her room to go to college and pulled out a senior picture of Leo and stuck on the back was this heartfelt poem. She hadn't seen that poem since her grandma died and what a coincidence that it was stuck to Leo's picture. She felt it was him sending her this message!

One day Sam was shaving in the bathroom with Leo's razor and reminiscing, remembering when Leo told him, "Dad you need to try this razor. It vibrates." As he was remembering that particular moment, the shaving cream bottle slid about five inches toward him. Sam thought it must be really wet so he put it back to see if it would slide again and, mind you, the bathroom sink isn't slanted. He even gave it a nudge, but it never moved. Once again, a sign from Leo to let his dad know that he is always around.

Coming back from Springfield in the car with Sam, Peter, and Filie, I was on the phone and Sam was trying to figure out who clapped. Thinking it was Filie or Peter he asked them and they said no, it wasn't them. They looked at each other and they realized it must have been Leo! It happened at the exact moment when Sam finished saying, "I wonder if Leo saw me at the scene, if his Spirit body was there hovering over us?"

Cheryl came into Leo's Pizza and told me her dream she had a few nights before: She was at a beautiful beach wedding with Leo, but didn't know who was getting married. Shortly after the ceremony, Leo was petting a dolphin and he was telling Cheryl to put her feet over the ledge and let them swim by. "It feels good and look, you can pet them!" Leo said. Cheryl thought the dream didn't make sense, but it made great sense to me! That same week of the dream, our families were supposed to be in Mexico at a resort that had dolphins you could pet, and my cousins were renewing their vows! Leo was trying to tell her that he was there! Awesome Message!

On July 18, 2014, we went to mass for Leo and Morgan's one-year memorial. After mass, we got a bite to eat and then went home. Cheryl called me to tell me that afternoon she had a vision of Leo and Morgan and my mom. She then asked, "Did you have problems with your pants this morning?" That shocked me because I did struggle in my room with my pants and even said, "God, don't let these pants rip open in church!" Cheryl said Leo showed her me struggling with my pants! I never said this to anyone. Sam was not around and Cheryl was in Pearl and didn't even know or see what I did that morning. So cool! Thank you my baby . . . Leo!

Cheryl called Sam on his birthday and asked, "What's up with the number 69?" She said Leo kept showing her the number 69 and thought it was hilarious! It's true Leo, Peter, Filie, and their cousin all knew this thing that Leo and his cousin always did: every time the number "69" would appear somewhere on signs, license plates, TV, pictures, etc., they would take a picture and send it to each other and thought it was funny. It was like a competition who could spot 69 the most. Previously that day, Sam asked Leo to show him some kind of sign. There it is! They're with us, just in the next dimension. This brought a chuckle to Sam and put a smile on his face.

It's April 14, 2018, and I'm not sure how to start writing about Leo and life after Leo. Maybe I should start from the beginning of his life? But before that, I'd like to say something about me. I have always believed that we each have our own destiny already pre-chosen before we are born here on earth. Now that's just my belief and the power of our free will has a lot to do with all our lives.

When Leo was born, I realize now and I believe his Soul knew, he would not be on this earth for long because Leo was fearless! When he was born, he had craniosynostosis, which means pre-suture closing of his skull. The skull would grow oval, not round. It was a cosmetic thing, nothing to do with the brain function. His brother Peter had the same thing seven years earlier. Peter had surgery with lots of complications and infections. When we heard Leo had the same thing, we decided not to do any surgeries. Instead, I went to church, got down on my knees, and asked God to watch over him as I do my other children, but with him, I was afraid when he got older, he might be ridiculed and bullied. So I told God I am putting Leo in his hands. As a mom, I was afraid for his future. Leo did grow up with a football-shaped head, but it was amazing watching him be so confident in himself and it was like he didn't have imperfections. Kids were always drawn to him and he never dealt with ridicule. I knew God had made him special, especially after his death—I put it all together! Because nowadays, there is no way a little boy with such a prominent abnormality would not be made fun of by other kids and not be hurt. I remember one day when he was in kindergarten and was playing in a corner with other kids and one of them called him football head. It went straight through my heart like a spike. I thought, "Here we go. It's already started," but I never said anything at school. When Leo came home, I casually asked him, "Leo, I overheard that kid call you football head. What was that all about?" He replied, "Mom, we all have names for each other. I call him lasagna." He laughed and I was relieved and amazed how confident and relaxed he was about it. I never mentioned it again until his teenage years and I saw him wear a t-shirt for soccer with a new nickname, "Eggo!" Again, I thought here we go. Now they are teenagers and maybe the teasing starts.

So I asked him again: "What is 'Eggo' about?" He replied very confident, "Well, my head is kind of oval, so they nicknamed me 'Eggo.'" As he was saying that, he was laughing and naturally was very proud of it and thought it was cool. That still shocked me, but I was relieved for him. He was a kid who never lacked friends from all walks of life.

When I look back after his death, I never realized how loved and influential he was with all his peers and even some older people.

The stories I have heard told to us after his death tell me that maybe that day when he was a baby and I prayed and told God that I was trusting and putting Leo in his hands, that was exactly what he did. Knowing his life was going to be short, God made sure that Leo was a good person and was going to leave a mark on this world by touching a lot of people before he died.

Two days after his death, we were going to go to the funeral home for preparations. Morgan's mom and dad stopped by our home because they were coming from the funeral home after making her arrangements. All four of us were standing in our foyer and Morgan's dad asked if they could bury Morgan next to Leo. My husband agreed right away. I almost said NO right away, but something inside said, "No, that's really rude. I'll think about it." I don't know why, but probably because my mind wasn't there yet, I was still in shock over it all! So within seconds I decided to say, "I need time," but as I was ready to say that phrase, I heard Leo in my right ear yell, "MOM, YOU BETTER SAY YES!" And I froze, thinking, "What in the hell?" Sam and Morgan's mom and dad were still staring at me waiting for an answer. Within seconds, I composed myself and realized that was "My Leo." I was not going crazy, and he did express his last wish and who was I not to oblige from that moment on. It was like our kids Leo and Morgan were happy that we realized and understood their wish to be buried together, and I can't explain it to this day! After that moment, I decided that if these funeral arrangements were the last thing I did for my Leo, I would make it the best as if I were preparing for his wedding! I swear, I felt them straight through it all, keeping me going! I will never forget his voice in my ear yelling those words! "MOM, YOU BETTER SAY YES! . . . YOU BETTER SAY YES!"

The day of the funeral was the second time I heard Leo's voice. After the church service, we were about to leave the cemetery to take people for the funeral dinner and we were in a hurry so we could get to Morgan's wake at the funeral home that afternoon. As I went to say goodbye to the casket where my beautiful Leo was going to rest in peace, I got down to kiss the casket and the moment I gave a kiss, I heard again in my right ear, "MOM, HURRY UP, LET'S GO, LET'S GO!" So I straightened up, looked down, and realized my Leo wanted me to hurry so I could get to Morgan's services. I ran to the truck and got in, as my husband thought I had gone crazy! I never said a word for my behavior; after all, there were still people standing around his casket, but I had to obey Leo's wish and didn't care about anyone else! I knew what I had heard and was waving my husband to hurry as well. Now that I think about that day, it seems if people were watching me (which I'm sure they were), they probably did think that I had lost my mind. But I know what I heard and I'd do it all again for Leo!

People may think it's wishful thinking, but I am a very grounded woman and I know each and every experience has been my Leo coming through to let us know that he is in a better place—and that one day we will be back together and that will be for ETERNITY!

—Tonia

The Contract

One day as I was sitting in Meditation, Spirit showed me a glimpse of my contract. It's the agreement I made while in my "Soul Group" on the Other Side before I was born.

Tonia and I were in this huge theater in the front row. We were sitting in these beautiful, white high-backed chairs. They were oversized and lined with red velvet. I saw the many buttons on the upholstery and the uniquely carved wood. The chairs hugged around us as we watched the screen in front of us.

Tonia was on the right and I was to the left of her. Her left arm and my right arm were intertwined as our fingers laced together. I could feel our hearts beating out of our chests. We looked at each other and both knew that we were about to watch something that was going to make our hearts stop.

As we sat there and were shown that Tonia would lose a child in this lifetime, we embraced each other as tight as we could as tears ran down our faces. As devastating as it was, we knew that by the "Grace of God" we would somehow, some way, make it through it! This was a way for Spirit to show us that we write our own story. We can't fully understand it. We can only trust that our Spirits are growing in a way we can't understand here.

As I was writing this piece, I was sitting out on my porch on a wicker loveseat. I had slid forward and put my feet up on the ottoman with my knees bent. I was so deep into the process that I didn't see the black snake that soon draped itself across my left ankle. I felt something softly touch my ankle, and I looked very nonchalantly down and there he was! He was about two inches or so around and six feet long or longer. I jumped up as I sat my right foot down and tossed him away with my left foot. I about had a heart attack. I'm afraid of snakes, but interestingly enough, he wasn't afraid of me. I was screaming and he slowly crawled off.

I believe in signs, but REALLY Spirit? Just show me a picture next time!

In Native American beliefs, the snake represents rebirth because of the shedding of the skin. The eyes cover over during the process and this is a symbol of increased clairvoyance. I was excited about the message because Tonia and I were preparing for a rebirth and could clearly see what was to come as we viewed it in that Spiritual Theater.

As I journey along this path, more doors open and I am learning as I go! It was important for me to understand that there is more growth to come. Clairvoyance is very helpful when we channel Spirit. It's visual and sometimes very detailed, which can make a big difference during a reading. I'm grateful for the sign the snake brought, but . . . REALLY Spirit? LOL!

Cheryl S. Kearns and Lacey Matthews (Photo by Melanie Miller)

Chapter 5

SPREAD YOUR WINGS

Lacey's Story

Life is full of ups, downs, twists, turns, speed bumps, and even U-turns. What happens when one single event changes life as you know it? The evening of July 17, 2013 happened to be one of those events for me. The tragic accident of Leo Alfano and his girlfriend changed life as I knew it.

I have to say that I knew for some time that I had some type of psychic abilities, but until that tragic accident I literally turned a blind eye to all of it. There were many times in my life I knew if I looked somewhere, I would see a Spirit or Ghost. I literally refused to look because I wanted nothing to do with it! I was scared of not only seeing Spirit, but of what doors might be flung wide open if I so much as cracked the door. So for years and years, I ignored this gift entirely and refused to acknowledge it even in the slightest. Never in a million years did I expect to be sitting here writing about this gift that took me a long time to view as a gift. I was completely fine ignoring it and burying my head in the sand. But Leo was adamant his family needed messages and flung the door wide open—the door I had tried to keep shut for so long. From that point forward, I could no longer ignore this gift.

This whole crazy journey started with my mother—remind me to thank her one day (not said sarcastically at all, LOL). My mom is not the same person she used to be. She was brought up in a household that went to church and was taught hellfire and damnation. I remember her not even wanting us to read our horoscopes as young kids. I, of course, found them fascinating and couldn't understand what was so wrong with it. I was also the child who wanted "special powers." I have always found the prospect of supernatural/psychic abilities intriguing. And yes, I am the same kid who as an adult turned away from all possibilities because they scared me. Isn't life interesting?

Anyway, my mom changed drastically around my junior year of high school. I remember having a migraine for over a month straight and my mom willing to do anything to find me some form of relief. After doctors upon doctors and medications upon medications had failed, she was ready to try anything. There was a man in our town who did Reiki and she scheduled me an appointment. During the session, one thing he said to me that will stay with me forever is, "I see you doing this kind of energy work one day." I didn't think much of it at the time, but looking back I know my path had actually started that day.

After high school, I went to college and met my husband Jelani. This man has been my support system more times than I can count. He didn't know the wild ride he was signing up for, but has done nothing but support me the entire time. We moved to Florida for five and a half years and had our first two children (Malik and Nevaeh) while living there. (We would later while in Illinois have our third child Kenyon). Later in the book, I will fill you in on their journeys (kids are amazing and highly intuitive). But what I will say for now is pay attention to your young children as they are way more connected to the Other Side than most even realize. While we were starting our lives together in Florida, my mom was in Illinois broadening horizons. She was starting to really connect spiritually. She took a class with Raymon Grace to learn dowsing, started taking yoga classes which led her to become a yoga teacher herself, and was seeing a holistic chiropractor who opened several spiritual facets. She was starting down her spiritual path and I didn't know at the time just how many doors she was opening for us both. Dang it, again I need to thank her! The story of her life is for her to tell, but had it not been for the doors she opened we wouldn't be where we are today.

During this crazy journey she set out on, she decided to open a day spa/salon/yoga center/healing arts center and so much more. My mom and I are more like sisters than mother and daughter. I was so excited for this amazing journey she was embarking on. I have an incredibly supportive father who wanted my mom to reach her dreams. She was turning life as they knew it upside down and he was there for her every step of the way. One day my mom called me and told me she had found a building she was going to buy in Jacksonville, Illinois to start her new business, Inner Harmony, and so the journey grew even more.

Right after the birth of Malik, I wanted to go to Massage Therapy School. I also have an incredibly supportive husband who doesn't blink when I say I want to achieve something. (After 16 years of being together he might be rethinking this—LOL!) My journey grew the day I enrolled in school. I never knew just how much this decision would change our lives. My mom started telling me she needed a massage therapist (this was her slight pushing suggestion we move back to Illinois). After the birth of our daughter Nevaeh in 2007, we were ready to move back. On New Year's Day in 2008, my parents came down and helped move us home. And I feel our journey grew far more than I realized this day.

Now before I get into this huge journey in Illinois, I want to backtrack to when I was a child. I stated before that I turned a blind eye to my abilities, but I can't recall exactly when that happened. I remember as a little girl being so very close to my great-grandma.

She was in an accident when I was young and sadly passed away. As I was so young, I don't remember much of this, but I do recall a few memories with her. I remember being very little and sitting on her countertop as she washed dishes. There was a window above her sink, and I remember the sun streaming in and wrapping around us. My legs were hanging over the countertop while I watched her work. I can honestly feel the warmth still to this day as I look back at this memory.

I also remember her dressing up in a pink colored wig for Halloween and me holding her hand as I skipped along, so excited for Halloween. I cherish these two memories more than anyone will ever understand. I loved her so much. She gave me a doll that had pink hair and as a child I naturally called her "pink hair." I remember after she passed, lying in bed saying my prayers, and then I would see great-grandma in my room and just talk to her. I didn't realize as a child she was a Spirit. She was there and I saw her just as if she were still here. I didn't realize this wasn't the normal thing. I know my abilities showed themselves way back then, even though as a child I didn't realize it. She has been there with me through this entire journey and always will be. I have to wonder what happened to make me shut those abilities off way back then. I doubt I will ever know, but I remember as a child how safe and peaceful she made me feel. I don't know exactly where this journey will take Mom and me, but I know my great-grandma will be right there.

When we moved back to Illinois, I started working for Mom at Inner Harmony as a massage therapist. My heart and Soul were into massage for the healing it provides others. I specialize in deep tissue, injury care, and hot and cold therapies. I love massage therapy because there is nothing better than being able to help clients who are in pain find relief. I thought back to the Reiki session I had in high school and how he said I would be doing energy work and I thought, "This is it!" But I now know it was just the beginning.

I incorporate a lot of modalities into my massage work, but I have come to learn that Spirit guides me. Clients will say, "How did you know exactly where I hurt even without me telling you?" Well it's not me, it's Spirit guiding me to where the pain is coming from and telling me how to work on it to alleviate it. My Spirit Guides are with me all the time and give me the knowledge of how to help others. There are downfalls to working with energy, though. It took me a long time to realize when you open yourself up to energy you can take on others "energetic stuff." I had to learn techniques to protect myself. Massage has opened so many doors for me that I didn't even know were there. How can you not want to help as many people as possible? And this leads me to where life started to really change! If there is a way for me to help others even a little, I want to do it! I have abilities I hid from and it was time to take down the armor, stop hiding, and start helping others even more.

Mom had already started embracing her gifts, but I was completely content to just quietly work with energy and kind of ignore the rest. Then the tragic accident happened and Leo pushed us to publicly share our gifts. Mom owned a business in a small town and we knew the ridicule that could follow us by publicly announcing it. But how do you not help a family in need? I am astounded daily by Spirit. They always bring through the healing messages that are needed. We are now offering private and group readings as Inner Harmony Mediums and are touched and blessed every single time Spirit brings through exactly what a family/loved one needs to be able to start to heal. I know the journey for Mom and me is still very much in progress, but I can't wait to see where Spirit takes us. I just continue to pray those who are hurting can receive even a small amount of healing. And I am beyond thankful Spirit has allowed us the immense honor of being able to deliver their healing messages to those who need them.

I want to thank my mother. This hasn't always been an easy journey and if it wasn't for her, I wouldn't be the person I am today. She has shown me how to have strength and to trust the journey. I am beyond thankful and blessed for such an amazing mom! Thank you for being the incredible, caring, loving person you are. I love you beyond words.

The Process

Lacey and I have been asked many times what it's like to talk to Spirit. People are curious about the process and how it works. Many are afraid to have anything to do with it because they believe it could be connected to the dark side. To be honest, the fear that I had and placed on Lacey at an early age was one and the same.

One of the first things Spirit let us know was the fact that we are protected by our Spirit Guides and Angels. They do all the heavy lifting on keeping the dark or so-called evil spirits at bay! It was one of our top concerns in the beginning, but our worries were completely put to rest.

I remember one of our first group readings where I saw a crime scene with the police tape around the area where it happened. I immediately became a bit anxious. Lacey could taste blood! We were newbies and as this began to unfold, we were in a state of almost disbelief. As the reading kept unfolding and Spirit kept giving us detailed messages, we kept delivering them. I remember Lacey was rocking a baby from the Spirit World. We kept looking at each other in utter shock. It was a multiple murder and suicide. The murderer sent messages through our Angels and Spirit Guides. We never spoke to him directly—they kept him a very safe and comfortable distance from us. He had messages that the family needed to hear for the sake of their healing. Our human side was very skeptical, but as Spirit brought the messages, it was clear that it was what they all needed to hear. In an instance like this we are very gentle on our delivery, but the thing we know and trust is we MUST deliver all of the message.

Readings

Just recently I took Lacey and Cathy to see a Medium at a group event. We wanted to see how she delivered her messages. We are always open to learning. What we learned was what NOT to do. As she connected to her Spirit Guides, she was very showy as she listened and responded. Then she began to deliver the message to someone in the audience. She then stopped and said, "Oh, no, I'm not delivering that," to the Spirit she was channeling.

What? Wait a minute! There is no way Lacey and I would ever do that. We trust and believe our Angels and Spirit Guides, so if they give us a message, we deliver it. The piece that we picked up that was positive is she asked us to take out a pen and paper so we could jot information down. This way you could read your notes later to see if you missed something. When you are getting a reading sometimes you miss the obvious. We call it "Reading Amnesia." Money well spent as we learned what to do and what not to do!

Another observation was her lack of compassion and not staying with a person when it was crucial. Compassion isn't something you practice, it's just who you are. Maybe it's the difference of Guides or how we all receive messages, but for us, we try to be as kind and gentle as we can while reading for someone.

It is different in a group when so many Spirits are trying to get through with a message. This is why so many times in a group, Spirit will deliver what we call "Piggyback Messages." This is where several people get some kind of connection from one message. Let's say Spirit shows us a beach ball. It might be that someone just bought a beach ball, someone is going to the beach, or someone else is going on vacation. The message can be multifaceted. So it is correct for all of them. Spirit does this for the sake of time.

Many times when we sit down to do a private reading for someone and they are desperate to hear from a certain loved one, they are shocked if another Spirit comes through that isn't that significant to them. For us it is usually an ice breaker. Spirit will hold the door to allow the secondary Spirit to enter first to help the person we are reading for to settle in and get comfortable before the Spirit that they really need to hear from comes through. Spirit always knows what we need and who we need to hear from. We do our best to tune in to their frequency to deliver the clearest message possible. It's like tuning in to a radio station. If it is 98.7 and we tune in to 98.1, it's just not as clear of a connection.

Some Spirits are easier for us to read than others. We have no idea why this is, we just do our best to get as much information as possible delivered. Spirit has to lower their frequency as we do our best to raise ours so we can meet on some common level to interact and do our job of delivering the best possible message.

Lacey and I were talking the other day about our first large group reading. We had 40-50 people show up. We were pretty nervous since it was our first group. Lacey had brought her Angel cards to enhance on the experience. Some people need to see what Spirit is conveying. It's like putting an exclamation point on a statement! I think it was a two-hour reading that day. It really seemed to have gone pretty well. The big lesson that we learned is you will always have a skeptic. There was this tall middle-aged man who seemed very, I don't know if odd or skeptical would be a better word. After we were done and we were discussing how it went to each other, Lacey spoke up and said she had a weird thing come through so she didn't share it. I chimed in and said I did, too. What Spirit showed her was bottle caps or jacks and I heard tricks or Trix? We laughed and said he probably had bottle caps or jacks in his pocket and was trying to trick us—along with the bottle caps or jacks he might of had Trix cereal in there. We got a good laugh, but it taught us to just deliver it all because someone needed to hear that!

Chapter 6

HEALING VISITATIONS

Sam's Story

On July 18, 2013, Sam lost his youngest son Leo. Leo left his earth home on that day, but he is around Sam all of the time.

I was at my grandson Malik's soccer game and "Counting Stars" came across the sound system. That is one of the ways Leo lets me know he has a message to deliver. When I sent the text to Tonia, she said Sam was on the phone with the doctor at that time getting results from some test. Leo let me know that Sam was going to be okay. He said, "I got your back Dad!" He always laughs and says, "You know I'm your favorite!" He is so darn cocky that he laughs at himself.

Even as we were sitting down for this interview, he talked about tractor tires. Sam said he was having issues with the tires on his tractor. I said he showed me boat oars. Sam laughed and said he had just told Peter that he had to get the boat out of the lake by next week before the lake closes. Every day when Sam gets up, he asks Leo, "So what are we doing today?" Sam feels Leo around him all of the time. He said if anyone saw him, they would think he was talking into a Bluetooth, but he is just talking to Leo!

On July 17, the night of the accident, Sam was up all night crying. He stayed at the house because so many people showed up. Tonia stayed at the funeral home with Leo. Sam said, "All I could say was 'My Leo is gone!'"

It was about 12:30 or 1:00 in the morning and there were probably 100 people at the house. Sam had an awful headache from crying. He decided to lay down on the couch for a few minutes. They had taken Leo's girlfriend Morgan to Springfield to the hospital. Sam said he fell asleep immediately when he laid down. He began to have a dream—or what we call a "Visitation Dream," which is where you feel like you are physically there. Every hour before he laid down, he had been calling the hospital to check on Morgan.

In his dream, he was in his shed and bent over working on a small engine. There was an air compressor by him with a hose attached. The end came off and the hose was whipping all around and he was trying to grab it. Sam thought, "What the shit." As he was frantically trying to grab the hose, he heard Leo behind him saying, "It's okay, Dad. Morgan just came unplugged!" Sam turned around and Leo and Morgan were about five feet away from him. Leo smiled and came over and put his hand on Sam's shoulder and said, "It's okay, Dad. I got her!"

Sam thought, "Don't you think we need to plug her in?" but he couldn't get the words out!

He had only been asleep about 10-15 minutes. When he woke up, he sat straight up and called the hospital. Morgan's sister said they had just unplugged her. It was happening as he had the dream!

When we have a dream that is this tangible, you know it's a visit from Spirit. We can feel them through a Spirit-type of physical touch. These are the best dreams of all! Sam knew Leo would take care of Morgan.

Ask and you shall receive . . .

Sam had a hunting trip planned in October to take Leo to Canada. He had planned it before Leo passed. Sam wanted to cancel the trip, but decided to go ahead and go. Peter, Sam, and some hunting buddies headed out. Leo and Sam had bunked together the year before. So many memories and so many tears. This was a really tough trip for Sam to take. Sam asked Leo to send him a sign. As he cried, he said, "God, Leo, I need a sign! Just send an orb in a picture or anything!"

They got up the next morning for the hunt and Peter shot a moose. Sam hadn't thought about his plea to Leo from the night before.

It was starting to snow and they pulled over to relieve themselves. Peter said, "Come on, Dad. Let's get some pictures while we are stopped." They took three or four pictures and then they got a call from the lodge that supper was ready. They got in the truck and headed back to the lodge.

When they got back, they grabbed the camera. In the three pictures of Sam and Peter, you could see "Leo" as an orb between Sam and Peter. Sam said, "Look Pete. It's Leo." Peter said, "Where?" Sam replied, "Right there, the orb!" They were both crying and called Tonia. It scared her—she thought something was wrong. Sam said, "You won't believe what Leo just did!" Sam added, "All I have to do is just ask Leo for a sign and he never disappoints!"

Sam gets signs from Leo almost daily. Sam will just ask and Leo delivers! One day Sam said, "Morgan, why don't I hear from you?" He wanted her to bring him a sign that she was okay. It was early September and Sam and Peter decided to finish the deer blind that they had started building with Leo.

It was a beautiful fall day. Sam loaded the tools on the trailer and hooked it up to the four-wheeler. He headed out to the middle of the cornfield. It was about a 20-acre cornfield and there was not a house for over a mile. Leo had chosen the spot earlier that year and planted a deer plot of clover about 100 x 100 square. There was a path to the plot and Sam was alone as he set out to it. As he was unloading the trailer, he heard a woman's voice as clear as day say, "Hello Sam!" He spoke out and said, "Who's in this cornfield? Where are you at?" He got quiet to see if he heard anything else. He was replaying it in his mind and he knew that voice. He called out, "Morgan Fair Child, it's about time you came and said hi!" How she said hello was the way she always said it to Sam, and he always called her Morgan Fair Child! This put a smile on Sam's heart to finally hear from her.

Sam was mowing one day with his head phones on. Tonia had told Sam that Morgan's parents had separated. Sam started having a conversation with Morgan. He told Morgan it was a good thing she wasn't here to see it. He said, "I'm sorry to hear about it."

After he was done mowing, he came in the house and laid down, and as he was watching TV he fell asleep. He started dreaming that he was on a bus trip with a bunch of kids. Morgan was there right next to Sam and Leo was in the distance. There were a lot of people on this trip. They were in a bus that was going up the mountain. As the bus went up the mountain, he could look out and it overlooked Cinisi Sicily, Italy, which is Tonia's hometown.

The bus pulled over to take a break about three-fourths of the way up the mountain. Sam kept wondering and asking, "Where's Leo?" Morgan never spoke in the dream. All of a sudden, the bus turned into Vespas (scooters).

Sam told Morgan that they needed to go find a hotel for the night because it was getting late. They kept looking, but the rooms were all booked up. Sam was looking at the sun and just like in the cartoons, it immediately sank. It was dark and Sam was desperately trying to figure out where they would sleep. Sam told Morgan, "We might have to sleep on these rocks." Again, Morgan never spoke. Then all of a sudden, they were in Sam's house in the states. They were at home in Illinois on Sam's couch. When Leo was a little boy, he would crawl up on Sam's chest and fall asleep, but this time it was Morgan. Sam just stroked her hair as she lay there. Sam was happy to be home with Morgan, but she was sad.

Sam asked Morgan if she was sad because it was hard in Heaven. He thought she must be sad about being dead. He told her not to worry. It would be like with Leo and get better in time. She shook her head no. Sam asked her, "Are you was sad because your mom and dad are getting divorced?" She squeezed Sam really tight. Sam asked Morgan, "Do you want me to give your dad a hug?" She nodded yes!

That next day Sam called Morgan's dad to see if he could come over, and he did. Sam went and gave her dad that hug from Morgan!

Ambassadors

Leo's dad Sam often asked me, "What does Leo do up there all day in Heaven?"

I always hated when he asked me that because I didn't have a definite answer. I told him he was my Spirit Guide and that was probably a full-time job! I'm sure I'm a full load for anyone to work with! Spirit has its hands full.

One day in August, 2014 when I was driving home from work, I was coming into the first curve out of Milton. Leo popped in as I was approaching the curve. A couple of weeks prior to this, a woman in her early 20s had a wreck and died on this curve.

Leo began to tell me, "Hey, tell my dad we are Ambassadors for the young who pass." I was taken by surprise, but quite relieved that I finally could tell his dad what Leo did in Heaven as a job!

Leo said many times children and young people are confused and scared when they first cross. Leo is there to help them cross over and show them the way. As usual, he is a Rockstar and he is helping his girlfriend Morgan learn this trade. Leo just seems to be good at whatever he attempts. What I know is that the young people are in good hands!

Sam was in Italy when I got this message from Leo, so I sent him a text. Sam picked up the phone and immediately called me. Sam was so excited to hear this. He always loves getting messages from Leo, no matter where he is or what he is doing. Leo delivers again!

Peter's Story

Leo is so good to come through for his brother Peter, with signs that he is still with him. Peter began telling me about going into a gas station and looking down and the candy bar price was 69 cents. Peter laughed and said that was Leo's number. It was a running joke with these boys and a couple of his friends about the number 69. He has even bombarded me with that number. Peter says everywhere he looks: candy bar 69 cents, the price of gas $2.69, and mile marker 69 on the road. Sixty-nine just pops up everywhere for Peter.

Peter has dreams of Leo, but they are very real—visitation dreams. These dreams are when you can actually feel the person as if they are here.

About a month or so after Leo passed, Pete had a dream where he was driving and stopped at a stoplight. He looked to his right and there was a police station. He felt very compelled to go in. His friend was behind the desk. He asked him what he was doing there. Peter asked if Leo was there and if he could have him back. Leo was there and said, "What's up Pete?" He was wearing a black t-shirt and jeans. Peter asked Leo, "What are you doing? I came to take you home!" They walked side by side and Pete had his arm around Leo. There was a door on the left and Pete wanted to go in, but Leo stopped him and said, "No, No, No, Pete, don't go in that door!" They turned to the right and there was a long hallway that they approached quickly. There were birds and a set of doors that began to open and a Bright Gold Light. Leo stepped in front of him and Peter was going to follow him, but Leo stopped him. He said, "You can't go past this point." Peter said, "Let me go with you and hang out with you." Leo let him know it was not his time yet, but when it was, he could come through these doors! It was hard for Peter not to go, but he told Leo he would wait until it was his time.

Not long after they lost Leo, Peter was at the pizza place and there were only two other people there. There's a closet in the back where they store containers of mushrooms and other supplies. It was about 11:30 p.m. and all of a sudden, Peter heard things falling off the shelf in that closet. Pete said he was sitting out front doing research on his phone when he heard the noise. We both laughed, and I said, "Sure you were!" (Momma Tonia just might read this!)

One of their employees was out front mopping and Pete said, "Did you hear that?" Peter was hoping that he heard it, but he didn't hear anything. Pete went back to check the closet and there were containers everywhere. He cleaned up the mess and went across the room to the adjoining room with the ovens to check on a pizza. Across from the ovens is the "make table" where they make the pizzas. Peter heard a coin hit the table as if someone had thrown it, but no one was around! He looked at one of the workers and asked him if he heard that, but he didn't hear it.

Peter found a penny across the room by the step that goes into the other kitchen, which is a decent distance from the make table. Needless to say, he still has that penny that he knows Leo threw at him!

One day at their home, Peter and his cousin were watching TV and all of a sudden most of the many pictures on the piano fell over and off the piano. Then later that night they were sitting at the dining room table and they heard the shower down the hall come on. They went to look and the shower was off, but the shower head was dripping and the floor was wet. Leo was at it again and they knew it when the cold chills went all over both of them. Too funny, because Leo was a clean freak and would sometimes shower twice a day. No surprise that Leo pulled that prank on them!

One night Peter was dreaming about sand volleyball. Leo was there, but there was an invisible glass between them. Peter would walk toward Leo, but he couldn't get to him. He kept trying to get to Leo, but kept running into the invisible glass. Pete kept trying to get his attention. Leo saw him and said, "Come on." Pete said, "I can't get to you!" Then Peter looked to his left and Leo was above him. There was a table there also. It was floating in front of Peter and above him. Pete was looking up at the table and there was a man sitting at it. He could only see his hands because his face was hidden from him. He had the knowingness that it was Jesus or God and the man told him, "Leo is fine!"

Peter's uncle passed away in October, 2017 and Peter had a dream they were all sitting around the kitchen table at their house. The family was all there—Peter, Leo, and their uncle—and they were telling stories, laughing about things they had done, such as hunting. They laughed and laughed and it was as if no one else was around. Peter told Leo that he wanted it to be just like in the movies and him coming back to visit.

In another dream, the family was at the house and Peter came in and said "Hi" to everyone. Leo and his uncle were there and Peter could see them, but his dad couldn't. He told Peter, "You can see me, but they can't!"

His uncle was kind of a serious guy. In Pete's dream, he was funny and sarcastic. He laughed a lot and told Pete, "You were one of my favorite nephews and you were 'the funniest one!'"

Leo always teased that he was the "favorite son." Well, right back at ya, Leo, because it sounds like Peter was the "favorite nephew!"

Peter talks to Leo all of the time. He has even asked him to send him a buck for deer season. Pete is still waiting on the big one. I told him that he needs to be more specific. Tell Leo how big and how many points and spread you want it to have because by now you have figured out Leo and his humor. I told Peter if you ask for a buck, he might send you a small button buck just for laughs.

After Peter and I finished his interview, he asked me if Leo was proud of him. He said he was looking at applying for a different job with benefits. I tuned into Leo and his response was so joyful for Peter. He told me he was "busting his buttons with pride!"

Peter laughed and said, "Look, Cheryl," as we were heading down the steps. He held his red and black flannel shirt that he was wearing like a jacket. He was missing a couple of buttons! As I gave Peter a hug, I again realized how amazing Leo is at getting messages through to his family and friends.

Some time has passed since we did this interview and Pete finally got that big buck. Leo never disappoints!

Filie's Story

The night after the accident, Filie fell asleep still in shock and wondering if Leo was okay! She was in a state of disbelief that day over the accident. Like anyone would do, she questioned God!

As she began to dream, she saw a large room with six to eight round tables. The room was filled with people she didn't know, yet they seemed familiar. It was as if she knew them in the dream.

She was laughing and, all of a sudden, she saw Leo in one of the chairs in front of her. Their eyes locked on each other and she began to cry. She hugged him and didn't want to let go.

Filie asked Leo, "What's Heaven like?" Leo replied, "Do you want to see it?" Filie said, "I can't go with you because my journey is not done yet!" Leo told her, "You don't have to, just look up!" He lifted his hands toward the sky with his thumbs together and palms open like wings. As he separated his hands, a Bright Gold Light came beaming down! He then closed his hands and said, "That's all I've got so far."

After this dream, four or five days passed and Filie didn't think twice about the room in the dream. Filie started hearing about a Spiritual Retreat that the Catholic Church puts on every year called Cursillo. This event is non-denominational: anyone of any religion or not is welcome to go. As a married couple, the husband has to go first, then the wife goes. People who have gone can sponsor you. Sam and Tonia, Filie's parents, had done it several years earlier before Leo passed.

Sam believes in God, but doesn't attend church very often. When Filie would hear her dad talk about going to Cursillo, he would say "If everyone would go to Cursillo, the world would be a better place." After someone has gone, they keep the process to themselves. After Leo died, Sam's words kept echoing in Filie's mind, telling her she should see what this is all about. She decided to do it that year.

After Sam and Tonia dropped her off, she walked into the chapel. She said she felt like she was in some kind of cult. Her next thought was, "What the hell am I doing here?"

Her parents dropped her off on Thursday evening and would pick her up on Sunday evening. On Saturday night the speaker got up from one of the chairs and began speaking about losing a brother. As Filie sat there listening, she realized the room looked so familiar to her, but there was no way she knew this place!

Then the speaker said something that made Filie laugh and she noticed the empty chair the speaker had been sitting in before. When Filie laughed and turned her head, it brought her back to that exact moment in her dream. She was having a déjà' vu moment. Leo was right in front of her in that empty chair at that very moment. It was the room from her dream that was exactly the same as the room she was sitting in at that moment! Filie and Leo locked eyes the exact same way and she began to cry uncontrollably.

After that experience, Filie would say she couldn't wait to go to sleep to see Leo. He would come to her in her dreams almost every night! He always knows what is about to happen.

One night, Leo's friend Colton was in her dream with Leo. Filie was about to say something to Leo about his friend Colton and Leo smirked and said, "I already know!" When Filie is dreaming and her alarm is about to go off, Leo will grab Filie and say, "Your alarm is about to go off!" Filie would hang on to him in the dream because she knew he had passed, but she didn't want to let him go!

Filie's mom Tonia would say, "I wish I could dream about him every night." She would say how much she wanted to see her son in a dream. Filie told her, "I don't think you could handle it." She would ask Filie every morning about her dreams. Then one night Tonia dreamed about Leo and when she woke up, she was so upset and depressed. She didn't want to leave her baby—she wanted to stay with him!

Filie constantly tells Leo not to scare her by coming to her bedroom or at least be in a well-lit area. She lets him know to only show himself if she is in a public place.

After Leo passed July 18, 2013, the family canceled their trip back home to Italy that year. The next summer in 2014 they took the trip. In the past, every year they would go with Leo there was a soccer match between the Italians and the Americans. This was always a "game on" and not always pretty for the Italian-Americans!

Filie didn't think they would continue this tradition and have a game that year without Leo. Their friend from Sicily said, "We should get a game going and do it for Leo." They were all in! Another friend got shirts made. The shirt design had Alfano 36 on the back and "In Memory of Leo" on the front. It took about two weeks to plan all of it. Before the game, Filie constantly got glimpses of Leo. She saw him 100 times or more, especially at the beach. She kept telling herself, "You are NOT seeing him!" She thought that she was going crazy, but what if he was trying . . . and she was really seeing him?

The day of the game, she was in the kitchen and her dad left to go run an errand. As Filie was in the kitchen, she thought she had heard a car pull up. She then heard the voice of her dad's sister, asking, "Where's Sam at?" Filie went to see her aunt to tell her that her dad was not there. Filie walked outside to look for her aunt, but there was no car and no one was in the driveway.

Filie knew that she had heard the distinct voice of her aunt. While having this feeling of an altered state as it impacted her in that moment, Filie looked up and captured a glimpse of Leo squatted down against the outside wall, wearing soccer shorts and shoes smiling at her—then he suddenly disappeared. She continued to look at the wall thinking she was crazy! Staying calm, she walked back into the house and into the kitchen. She knew she had seen her brother, but as she continued to repeat that to herself, the crazier she began to feel about the situation.

She walked slowly into the kitchen, pale and in shock. Filie's mom saw how she looked and began to freak out and asked her what was wrong with her. Filie thought "How do I say I just saw Leo?" She didn't know how to tell her mom and then she blurted, "I swear I'm not going crazy, but I just saw Leo!" Her mom froze and then said, "Of course I'm going to believe you!" This was the first time Filie saw Leo.

The second time Filie saw Leo, she saw him during the holidays. All holidays are hard for the family. Filie tries to be the strong one and keep everyone's morale up. She pushes herself to be positive for everyone else.

It was Christmas Eve, 2017 and her parents had fallen asleep on the couch. Filie was laying down watching TV, thinking about the holidays without Leo. She was crying and didn't want to wake her parents. She was so unbelievably sad that she cried herself to sleep. Hours later at 4:30 a.m. she woke up, not moving a muscle, just opening her eyes. She saw Leo across from her in the recliner that he always sat in. Their dog Achilles was sitting there looking up by the recliner.

Filie kept closing and opening her eyes and focusing on the chair, the dog, and Leo. She could see the dog's head move as Leo was petting him. She could see his coat press down as he was petting him. Leo was there! Filie sat up, not scared at all. She just sat there watching him. He was still there petting the dog and Leo said to her, "Merry Christmas, I love you!" Filie was frozen and then she laid back down, very happy that she got to see her brother. He always shows up when she needs him the most!

One night Filie met Leo in a dream. They were on their family boat and he was driving. It was a beautiful day on Lake Jacksonville. Filie was up front with Leo and he was all smiles.

A few days after this dream, Filie and her family took the boat out on the lake. Filie's dad Sam was driving. At one point, Sam left the driver's seat and Filie happened to look toward the back of the boat and realized that it was a déjà vu of the dream that she had earlier that week. Sam had vacated the driver's seat and when she turned around, everyone was in the same positions that they were in her dream. The chair was empty, but that was where Leo was sitting in her dream. Filie could see him as clearly in 3D form as if he were truly there! This wonderful déjà vu moment gave Filie a beautiful experience while awake, as if Leo was truly there in a physical form.

Filie gets messages from Spirit and she never hesitates to deliver the message—no matter how crazy someone might think it is.

Before her uncle passed of pancreatic cancer, the last month or two he got really bad. Filie's dad Sam was there taking care of his brother. Sam would go there and stay several weeks at a time.

One week after Sam's brother passed, Filie had a dream. Her uncle came to Filie and she asked how he was. He told her he was much better, but needed her to get a message to her dad.

Her uncle said, "I need you to tell your dad something for me. Although I was not able to convey how much I appreciated him, I know how much he took care of me, did for me, and supported me. Make sure he knows that I know he was there!"

Filie had a dream that she was in her dad's sister's house in Iowa. Her aunt has six boys and three of them were sitting on the couch with their mom. They were watching TV. To the left side of the TV is a hallway that leads to the bedrooms. All of a sudden, Leo came walking toward them. Only Filie could see him. She was so excited to see him, but he said, "Stop, this isn't for you. You have to deliver the message! Now listen, tell Aunt what I have to say!" Filie said, "Okay," and began to listen as Leo gave her the message. "You need to tell Aunt I have not left her side and I'm still here!" Filie said, "Yes," and Leo said, "No, you need to tell her. I'm here and haven't gone anywhere!" At this time, their aunt was battling breast cancer in real life.

Filie woke up and immediately got on Facebook and messaged her aunt the entire message. She finished by saying, "I don't know, but I hope this message can help you in some way!" Her aunt sent her a thumbs up emoji back. Filie didn't even respond because how do you take just a thumbs up?

The next day her aunt called Tonia, freaking out and was in more shock than Filie. She couldn't understand how Filie knew which three sons were on the couch with her while they were watching TV, let alone that she was sitting there that night asking Leo and his cousin on the Other Side, "So what? You two just leave me and don't come see me anymore?" Filie then realized, "Okay, I relayed the message!"

Now we can all understand how important it is to deliver messages from Spirit!

Who am I Really?

I am a child, a sister, a niece, an aunt, a daughter, a wife, a mother, a nana, a daughter-in-law, a friend, a hairdresser, a yoga teacher, a business owner, an entrepreneur, a medium. . . . The list can go on and on, but really I'm Spirit. A Soul having a Spiritual Experience in a physical body.

Let's not get in our heads too much over this, but my belief system is earth is our classroom and as we have experiences, we advance our Soul. So think of it this way: Think of a ladder with 100 rungs or a staircase with 100 steps, for example. As we face an experience and, let's say we accomplish it, we get to take a step up. The easier the experience, the fewer steps and the harder the experience, you gain a few more steps if you get the lesson that is involved.

Spirit has shown me this mystical staircase with a Soul on it that I am channeling, and I see them take a step. So yes, whether we are here or have crossed over, we are still evolving.

I do believe we evolve much quicker here on earth because it is so much harder. Keep in mind those on the Other Side who are helping us—who we are connected to—are evolving by helping. So it's a win-win when we get the lesson!

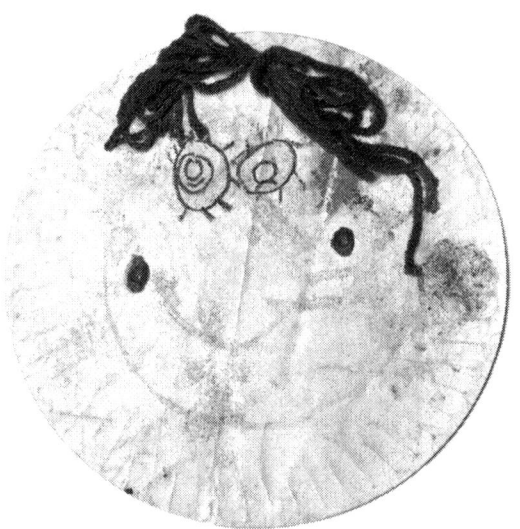

Paper Plate Angel (Photo by Melanie Miller)

Chapter 7

PAYING ATTENTION

Spirit Talks to Us in Many Forms

That moment you wake up from that dream, listen to that song, or experience it through dance. Many times, we are asked how we get our messages when we channel. Just like you, we watch for signs, we listen, and we pay attention.

Music is one of my personal favorites and I often wonder when the artist is writing the song if he or she knows Spirit is channeling it. The many facets that Spirit uses are fascinating.

Each of our sessions are unique on how we receive messages. Take for instance, when Lacey and I are meeting our friends and fellow Mediums Deb and Todd to read for each other, you never know what might happen. I remember waking up in the middle of the night and Deb's son Andy who had passed October 16, 2010 (a few years prior to us meeting) came through like rapid fire at 2:00 in the morning. He gave me a list of ten things. I quickly grabbed something to write them down for our session later that day. Andy was so excited that we were getting together to read each other. We joined Deb and Todd later that day and Andy came through with flying colors, but it was nice to have his list to add to the experience.

At first, I was hesitant to tell those whom I was reading for if Spirit gave me something odd to deliver. In Andy's case, it was knee pads.

I told Deb and she said they bought him knee pads when he got where he couldn't walk: he walked on his knees. Boy, was I relieved for that validation. The next day after we got together, I was behind an SUV with the license plates ANDY1. Thanks again, Andy!

Okay, so here are a few ways that we roll. Sometimes we actually see Spirits 3D, which is *clairvoyance*. Some come through as snapshots in our mind's eye. Sometimes we feel them and their stuff—*clairsentience*. Sometimes we just have a knowingness and that ability is known as *claircognianze*. Yes, and sometimes we hear them—*clairaudience*. Each session is different, just like each of us has a unique personality as do they and the ability to communicate is unique. It's like tuning in to a radio station: when you are right on the station it is as clear as a bell, but if you are slightly off, just a little, the signal isn't quite as clear. We try to tune in the best we can to get as good of a reading as possible. It's all about helping Souls to heal.

When the four of us get together, it is interesting, to say the least. We all have our strong suits and we support each other with our validation. It's never a dull moment when Lacey, Deb, Todd, and I have a Spirit session!

From the moment we met, we all had an immediate connection. Deb and I laugh and call each other "Soul Sister!"

Michael

When the movie *Michael* came out, I was watching it at home. We had gone to the theater to see it and I loved it. So when it came on TV and video I was so excited to watch it over and over. I have always been drawn to "Archangel Michael." After watching it, I shut my eyes and the next thing I hear as I had fallen into that meditative space was, "You watched the movie!"

I sat straight up to see who said that in my ear. Ben was not home yet. He was still farming and I was home alone. This really kind of freaked me out. The strange thing is, I knew it was Archangel Michael!

Paying Attention 73

A strong male voice that was so convincing. I kept trying to dismiss it, but to this day, I can feel the presence it had. It felt like sacred ground. Another way for Spirit to get my attention and drive it home!

Spirit can communicate to us in many forms.

- *Clairaudience:* When we hear Spirit. It can be external like Michael did with me or it can be an internal hearing.
- *Clairvoyance:* When we see Spirit. This can be an actual 3D experience. You can also see a picture in your mind's eye or a short slide show or a movie clip, so to speak.
- *Clairsentience:* The ability to feel Spirit. Many times, a Spirit will give us a sensation in our body that connects to an ailment or even the sense of a lost limb or being intubated.
- *Claircognianze:* The ability of knowingness. It's when you know it, but you have no prior knowledge of it. But you just know.

When we channel Spirit, we never know how they are going to convey their message. It's always a surprise and it keeps life interesting!

Angelic Music

One day at my house, my older sister and Lacey were hanging out in my dining room. We had all taken classes and were interested in Energy Work. We were sitting and talking about different experiences when all of a sudden, we smelled jasmine and heard Angelic Music. We stopped talking and looked at each other very surprised! Of course, our question to each other was, "Did you hear that?" and "Did you smell that?" We all confirmed the same experience. That was really cool and a bit freaky at the same time. When you first start paying attention and acknowledging Spirit, it is as if the flood gates open. You have to learn to trust what you hear, see, smell, feel, and so on. This helped us all because I didn't have any flowers blooming or music playing. Spirit is just amazing like that. When you trust and believe, it is phenomenal!

Pay Attention to the Signs

One of the things we tell the person we do a reading for is to pay attention because after a reading, Spirit is so excited that he or she made the choice to get a reading to connect with them that they will flood them with signs. It's kind of like walking into a dark room. You are in the room, but you can't see what's around you. Once the light is turned on, you see things clearly in the room. I wonder how many people keep walking into that dark room, afraid to turn on the light?

Signs are a gift from our loved ones on the Other Side. Let me share a few of the signs that Spirit comes through with.

- *Coins:* When you all of a sudden start finding coins, it might be the same coin such as only dimes or only pennies, or it just might be coins in general. I laugh and tell my loved ones to drop me $100 bills! They just appear in the oddest places and right under your nose. Check out the date on the coin or add the amount up to see if those mean something special. But know Spirit is just letting you know they are there with you.
- *Birds/Animals:* You start to notice the same bird or animal repeatedly, but they seem to pop out at every turn. My grandma shows up as a female redbird. When I see one, I know she is there. I must tell you what happened when I went for a reading with my friend Deb. Grandma came through at the reading that she would show me redbirds as a sign of when she is around. After the reading, I stayed at my business (Inner Harmony) where I have a deck upstairs. My friend Cathy and I were sitting out there and a female redbird landed on the deck fence just singing her lungs out. A few days later, two more female red-

birds landed on my fence, chatting it up. Then a day later, one landed on the fence and hopped down on my water fountain as she chattered, took a drink, and I said, "Thanks Grandma." After I acknowledged her, that was the last visit! What you need to understand is I had never seen a redbird on my deck before or since. I got the message and acknowledged Spirit which was the message I needed. She was teaching me to see signs from our loved ones. Grandma always says hello through the redbird and I am grateful!

- *Songs:* This is one of my all-time favorite ways to get a message. When Lacey and I are in a session doing a reading, it never fails that Spirit comes through with a song of significance. Sometimes it describes them, sometimes it was "their song," sometimes it depicts an era or place they heard it play. Also, the lyrics can simply tell them what they need to hear. It never fails! Sometimes it points to the artist that the deceased or living loved. Lacey just rolls her eyes when Spirit has me sing it. It puts joy in my heart, with a side of laughter. It's good for the Soul, you know!

- *Numbers:* Wow, this one can get tricky. Let's say we get the number 17. It could be their favorite number, they passed at the age of 17, it has been 17 years since they had passed, they passed on the 17th of the month, or on January 7 ("1" representing the first month and "7" representing the day of the month). Maybe this was their football jersey number or it took 17 days for them to pass. As you see, we must think outside the box and break it down sometimes. Repetitive numbers are another way they get our attention. Have you ever just looked at the clock and it's the same time every time when you wake up on different days. You might see 3:33 in the afternoon or you wake up during the night and see that it is 3:33 over and over again. That is Spirit letting you know they are there or giving you a clue to a message.

- *Feathers:* When we find feathers, it is a sign our loved ones or Angels are with us. It is always when we are needing it the most, and it sure brightens our day. You will hear people say, "I find feathers all the time," and I always say, "Thank you Grandpa for letting me know you are with us," or whomever it might be!
- *Smells:* You might smell your loved one's cologne or a certain fragrance that they wore. You might smell cookies baking (but none are) and you know it's your grandma who always baked for you. They love to send their message through a smell. It might be tobacco or pipe smoke: they are pretty creative!
- *Glimpses:* Sometimes when we are what I call "in the zone" like a meditative state, you know, just staring off into space and you catch a glimpse of someone and you could swear it was your loved one who had just passed. Know that's another way of Spirit getting your attention. The first time this happens, it can be hard and bring you to tears, but the more it happens, it begins to bring great comfort. Spirit is amazing at this type of sign and I love it!
- *Touches:* Have you ever felt like someone just touched the back of your hair . . . or you have a sensation on your skin? Those are gentle touches from Spirit. If you are very sensitive, you might feel presence of warmth or tingling of energy by your side. I'm so grateful for these sweet kisses from our Angels or loved ones!
- *Goosebumps:* When we are reading for someone and their loved one comes through with details and you deliver the message to them and they can confirm it, we will get goosebumps like crazy. Many times, they get them also. Don't you just love it when that happens?
- *Billboards and License Plates:* These are always fun. When your attention is drawn to words, titles, letters, anything that gets your attention out of the blue. That's Spirit. They have a way of using all of their resources.

As Mediums, we celebrate when the signs are being recognized as a message from Spirit. There are so many ways that they can communicate a full message through a simple sign. Spirit is very detailed to lay out the groundwork before a life-changing event. They work to prepare and teach us how to connect so we can survive what is to come.

Joyce's Story
"Drops of Jupiter"

I have always had a strong interest in mediums, tarot, readings, crystals, spirits, dream interpretation. You know, the stuff that gets you looked at like by some like you're crazy. I'm adding my story so others may see how our journey is to help and be helped, love and be loved, see and be seen, and to understand we are never alone and we are never gone.

I will begin with the recollection of driving to work the 18th of July, 2013, and saw several people and flowers at the corner of the gas station south of Jacksonville. I said a prayer and thought how tragic, not knowing at the time what had happened and how this would later tie to me. I learned later in the day while at work, that one of our customers had lost his nephew in a motorcycle accident: the young man Leo and his girlfriend Morgan had been killed. And so begins the connection and part of what brought me to Cheryl and Inner Harmony Mediums.

I had been to a reading several years ago with a lady who came to a hotel in Jacksonville. During that reading, she said we ALL have the ability to read and understand messages. I wanted to do readings and get messages. She had told me during that reading she saw five in our family. At that time, it was just myself, my husband Ebert, and our son Jesse. No way was I ever considering having another child. This would have been around 1988 at the time. Time passes, we change, and in 1992, I had another son Sean and then Jacob was born in 1994. So her reading was accurate and the accuracy reinforced my desire to read and understand messages.

I had already experienced great loss in my family. I had lost my dad in August, 1997, my half-sister in November, 2005, my mom November, 2010, and then my aunt May, 2013. I knew Mom was always with me and I talked to her often. My aunt always loved redbirds and when I saw two of them together, I knew it was Mom and Aunt Helen saying "hi" and that message made me smile.

I came across something in the newspaper about Inner Harmony offering readings in Jacksonville. JACKPOT! I was feeling lost over Mom's and my aunt's passing. I wanted to find out if I could learn to read so I was super excited to know there was someone in Jacksonville I could go visit. I had been having pain in my right forearm and thought the reading could help: all things tie together. Yes, I'll go for a reading before I go to a doctor. I scheduled a private reading with Cheryl and Lacey. I had never met either one and didn't know if this was a scam or what was up. I was very guarded. I don't know what I was looking for in that first reading—a miracle answer, an instant fix, the light to go on and all my problems to be solved—but what I did find was someone who saw into my Soul and became a very dear and valued friend. This reading opened up so much.

During that first reading, as I said, I was very guarded. It's hard to help someone or read them when they have a wall up; and our ego builds walls. Cheryl and Lacey talked with me, quizzed me, and scribbled in their books. They both picked up on the women in my family who were with me and helping me, guiding me, sending me messages—mainly my mother, my grandmother, and my aunt. I told them about the redbirds and knew they were messages from my aunt and mom. They told me to pay attention to the things around me and watch for the messages. I'm a crier—always have been, always will be—everybody was crying by the time I left. When I was pulling out of the parking lot, I looked up and saw these two jet streams crossing the sky, looking a *little farther out I saw the third: that was my confirmation. My first "ah-ha" moment. Had I seen signs before? Yes. Had I just received confirmation? YES!*

I attended Cheryl and Lacey's first group reading and learned the history of Leo and Morgan. Leo's mother, Tonia, was attending and my mind went back to the site of the accident and how our paths cross and no meeting is by chance. I listened to the stories of how Leo messaged Cheryl and Lacey, prodding them to share their gifts. I cried and smiled over the story of the cross necklace Tonia struggled with, but hadn't shared with anyone. Did she keep it or bury it with her son? Leo communicated with Cheryl and Lacey that his mother needed to keep that cross necklace. The message left such a feeling of relief.

I shared my experience with my son Jesse and his girlfriend Katy. Jesse and I shared lots of similar likes—maybe I taught him mine—Halloween, my "weird" beliefs, power of positive thinking, ask, believe, receive, get someone to smile or laugh, movies, etc. So sharing this with him was nothing unusual. I asked if he'd like to go to a reading. He and Katy both said they would love to go. Katy was especially interested as she had lost her grandmother whom she was very close to and she thought it would be helpful.

I think the first group reading Jesse and Katy accompanied me on was late October or early November, 2013. I don't recall all the details of the reading, but the messages given were healing and sparked more interest. During that reading, I recall one thing specifically that was given to Jesse and Katy and that was the number two. At that time, Jesse and Katy were engaged to be married June 7, 2014 and thought it could relate to number of children. Charlie had been born July, 2012, so we chalked it up to another child. One thing I gathered from the readings, you don't always get the answer to a specific question, but you get responses. You will take something away that is what you need, something that is beneficial; however, it sometimes seems like a disappointment because it wasn't the person or answer you were seeking.

I started taking yoga classes with Cheryl and continued going to readings, mainly group readings. In November, 2013, I lost my niece to cancer and 13 days later, my nephew due to a heart attack. Was this part of the "two" message? I continued yoga, readings, and visiting with Cheryl and Lacey when I went for my haircuts and nail appointments. Somewhere in the mix of time, I even started working every other Saturday at Inner Harmony; best job I ever had!

During my time at Inner Harmony, I had a dream (several actually) and related them to Cheryl. One in particular was a very upsetting dream. I was on a road and driving. I recalled two vehicles whizzing past and then an ambulance came careening up, almost hit me, swerved and then ended up turning over on its side, wrecking. Between that dream and the continual dreams about storms and tornados, both Cheryl and I interpreted the dreams as a major change was about to occur in my life.

So you ask, what do the ramblings of this woman have to do with readings, healing messages and, of all things, "Drops of Jupiter?" August 18, 2014 and Jesse Dale Coates. A phone call from Katy at 5:34 that Jesse had collapsed at work and they had taken him to the hospital. I hurried to get ready to make the drive to Louisiana, Missouri and somewhere in that time, a thought, "There is nothing you can do." Ebert was driving a truck for a local trucking company and making a delivery in Michigan. I called him when I pulled out of the driveway that Jesse had collapsed at work and I was on my way to the hospital. On my way to the hospital, I was numb, unseeing, just driving until I noticed a huge flock of white birds take off toward the blue sky. I can still see their flight, Heaven bound.

Katy met me in the hospital lobby as I was walking in and she just shook her head. My throat constricted, my chest tightened, my fists clinched, and my heart broke in two and then the heart-wrenching scream of "NO" was all I could repeat. Jesse had turned 31 on the 6th of August. He had been sober ten years and married just two months.

Jesse left behind two: a wife and child—Katy and Charlie (who had turned two in July). He also left behind two brothers, two parents, two in-laws, two grandparents. The two number . . . TWO.

Jesse wasted no time in sending me his first message. I had stepped outside to call Ebert and tell him his oldest son has passed away and as I collected myself, I saw a young man of similar build to Jesse walking up to the hospital. He was wearing scrubs and as he got closer, I noticed his shirt. It was dark blue with motorcycles. He walked up to me and asked if I was okay. I told him no, that my son had just passed away, but had to smile thru tears for the first time as I patted his motorcycle-covered chest and accepted his sympathy.

Maneuvering thru the week that followed was very difficult. We had the support of Jesse's many friends and family. We held a celebration of life party at our home Saturday, August 23, after Jesse had passed. Cheryl came to share Jesse's first "hey there." Cheryl told me after she had left the memorial service on Thursday, she'd stopped at a fast food restaurant to get a bite to eat. While sitting in the drive thru, Cheryl said she looked in her rearview mirror and looked down at the memorial flyer back to the rearview mirror because the guy in the truck behind her looked just like Jesse. I don't recall now how Cheryl communicated to me (text, at yoga class), but she told me when she left our house Saturday she had seen some dragonflies and then a song came on the radio—"Drops of Jupiter" by Train. At the time I couldn't recall the song. Cheryl told me it was a song Pat Monahan had written after his mother had passed. I listened to the song and, of course, I cried. That is Jesse's message song, and I mean message song. The song was written in 2001, the same year Jesse graduated from high school. This song is a communication between many. Everyone seems to know that this is MY song and Jesse is speaking to me. He uses this song to communicate with others, not just me.

I recall having bought a bottle of wine for a friend as a Christmas gift and could not find that bottle anywhere. I ran to the store in Green-

field to pick up another and drop that one off at a friend's house. While I was in the store looking at their limited wine selection, I see this "clearance" basket of wine. In the basket were "Save Me San Francisco" bottles of wine, "Drops of Jupiter" wine and "Calling All Angels." SIGN! I bought the wine and gave them as gifts: one for my friend, one for Cheryl, and one for me.

I normally stopped at the gas station as I was headed home from work. I stopped one winter night after yoga class. When I pulled up to the car next to me, I could see a gas can next to the car and a young man sitting in the car. Written on the back window was something about hugs, given freely, something along those lines. The car was filled to the gills. A young lady was standing next to the car and as I got out and started inside, I said to her, "Is there anything I can help you with?" She said a pack of cigarettes would be great. I went in, got my usual lottery ticket and a couple of packs of smokes. I went back out with the cigarettes and asked if they needed gas. She was reluctant to say yes. I told her to have her boyfriend pull up to the pump and fill the car with gas. He did so and I went back in to pay, got them some food and bottled water for the road, and then went back out to give her the bag. She said thanks and asked can I get your name . . . told her mine, Joyce, and what was hers . . . Grace . . . saved by grace was all I could think . . . we shared a hug or two and I wished her well. I drove off toward home and thought about Jesse . . . help somebody if you can . . . and then "Drops of Jupiter" played on the radio. You did good, Mom.

We lost a very good friend not far from our home in an auto accident. Jesse and Ebert coached him in junior football. He and our son Sean were best of friends and he was coming to our house the night of the accident. There is a cross at the spot where the car ran off the road and he passed on June 9. It was especially difficult to drive by that cross on the one-year anniversary of his passing. I had made several trips into town that day and thought of him each time I went by, but the last trip home of the night Ebert was with me. I had been remembering

Jesse and our friend during junior football league. I knew what his mom was dealing with and my heart hurt for her: another mother who had lost her son. As I rounded the curve and approached that cross, "Drops of Jupiter" began its dum dumdumdum and the sob escaped and the tears rolled. That was the first time I think Ebert experienced and understood the "Drops of Jupiter" message!

As crazy as it sounds, Jesse has impeccable timing. Believe what you want, I believe he speaks to me through that song and many other ways: coins, feathers, birds, billboards, license plates, signs on trucks, all forms of communication. I take the messages he sends with love and gratitude. I know there is so much more to this life: things beyond our understanding and our physical limitations, yet things we are intended to learn and experience. Always be open to love, learn, and experience this vibration we call life. The vibration does go on. It is limitless and timeless as is the communication. Take time to listen for your own "Drops of Jupiter." And always say Thank You!

—Joyce

Penny for Your Thoughts

Most of us have heard the saying, "a penny for your thoughts," but have you ever paid attention to what you were thinking when you find that coin? Who were you thinking about? Was it an inspirational thought? Did you just do or say something that needs a special acknowledgment?

I used to find pennies in various locations: "Always gotta be heads up before you pick it up"; "Lucky penny in your shoe, pick it up, you'll have good luck all day." When I used to find pennies, I'd kick them if they weren't heads up, until they flipped over. I'm sure I got stares from onlookers thinking what is that goof in the parking lot kicking and chasing around. Now, I no longer worry about which side is up. I take them as messages and say thank you!

My friends and family know I find change on a regular basis. My left shoe always has at least two pennies. Sometimes by the end of the day, I may have several pennies, dimes, nickels, or quarters in my shoe. My son Sean's fiancé, Amber, was going to get a pair of shoes for me as a Christmas gift. Amber didn't want to rifle through my closet to find out my shoe size, so she sent Sean in to find out. He came back and reported, "Well, I think she wears a size seven and I'm not sure what's up, but all her shoes have money in them!"

Yes, I find change. More importantly, I find messages. I think about Jesse often and give him a good portion of the credit for the change I find. Jesse usually tosses pennies in groups of two. But there are others that I credit, too. If I find a nickel, that's for my cousin's son who was nicknamed Nickel. He was killed in a logging accident. I always make sure to send up a "Thanks, Nickel" because that was his nickname.

There are times it seems I just have a thought or a question running around in my mind and once I make a decision, I may find a coin—confirmation the universe heard me and agrees. It's unique, odd, coincidental, divine intervention, rare, illuminating, or quirky, but I always say thank you.

Most recently I found five pennies in the back yard of the house we are renting in Georgia. Why would I find five pennies in the grass, not to mention a place I'd walked over several times before and never noticed them? I picked up the pennies along with the cool rock mixed in with the find and took them in the house. I took a picture of my loot and sent it to Cheryl. I discovered my find connected me to Cheryl, who, as she said, was having a good cry at that moment. I was able to lighten her mood and gave her something else to focus on. It is nice knowing those coins helped a connection. Cheryl said I must have been a pirate in a past life. HaHa!

So pick up that coin, be aware of your thoughts, share your story, and say thank you. Remember, they are also pennies from Heaven.

—Joyce

Chapter 8

HEALING THE WOUNDED SOUL

Feeling Desperate

It's sometimes a little tough to read for someone who is so desperate to hear from a certain loved one. They want it so badly that they block the process. We have them relax and take a few deep breaths. If that doesn't work, we have them take a drink of water. They are just too excited or nervous about the reading. It's okay and it always seems to work out. Spirit usually brings through someone else first and I think it is just to break the ice and hold the door open for the Spirit they are so desperate to hear from.

Sometimes the Spirit they want to hear from might not come through. Spirit knows just what we need to hear and who needs to deliver the healing message that we need at that point in time.

When Spirit comes through in a reading to let the family know that they are right there by their side, it brings such a blanket of peace to them that it is hard for me to put into words. I just know how grateful Lacey and I are during those moments for the family that we are reading for. It is such an honor for us to deliver the message.

Paula's Reading

I arrived at work on a Tuesday last Spring and Paula was getting her nails painted. I spoke as I entered the salon and she asked me if I was the owner. I told her I was and she said, "You and your daughter did a reading for me and it saved my life!"

This took me by surprise because I usually remember faces, but not names. As I looked at her, I remembered her face as she began to tell me her story.

We don't usually remember much about the readings we do. We are simply the messenger between the person we are reading for and Spirit.

Back in 1990, Paula's dad had just found out that he was denied for a heart transplant. About a month later, he did go into the hospital to get a pacemaker put in. He was a strong Christian man who loved his family and he didn't want to be a worry to his wife, so he had the procedure done.

He was in the hospital for a few days and came home on a Friday. Paula, her husband, and kids went to see him on Sunday. Being a Daddy's girl, she noticed her dad didn't seem like himself that day. He asked her if she was coming back the next day. She told him no—she had to work, but would come after work to see him.

The next day, Paula's dad committed suicide before she got there. Paula blamed herself, knowing that if she would have been there it wouldn't have happened.

She carried this guilt every day of her life. She was so depressed and sad that all she could do was muster up enough energy to get up and go to work. When she came home, she would go straight to bed. Doctors put her on antidepression medicine, but nothing worked.

Paula saw the article in the local newspaper about us doing readings. She thought she would like to try it. She called for prices and just knew her husband would think it was too costly since he took care of paying the bills.

She told her daughter Faith about her desire to come and asked her if she would be interested in going. Faith said she would.

Paula's birthday is on Christmas Eve and Faith surprised her with an early birthday gift. It was a gift certificate for a reading. She called and booked the appointment for Saturday, December 6, 2014.

When we sat down to do the reading, Lacey said, "There was an older male Spirit sitting at my kitchen table this morning reading the paper. He was very anxious to talk to Paula."

Her dad believed that there were Angels on earth—he had some experiences. He had been working on getting her to come for a reading and then he worked on Faith to get the pieces to fall together.

As we were channeling him, he raised his voice and said, "Out of all of our experiences together in your lifetime, you're letting this one define you?" He began to talk about the day he walked her down the aisle. He told her to remember the good memories! He began to talk about them living in their new home, which they got after he passed. He talked about her husband and his tractors. He let her know that he is still with them.

Paula told us that she felt like if she would have been there on that Monday that he wouldn't have committed suicide. When he came through at the reading he said that he had made up his mind. If not that day, he would have just done it another day.

Paula was scheduled to have knee surgery. She and her husband both had a dream that she died on the operating table. Neither one of them told each other about the dream until Paula finally mentioned it because she needed him to know about her life insurance.

Paula's dad came through at the reading and told her not to worry about the surgery because she would be fine! Faith reminded her mom, "Remember, Grandpa said it would be okay." She had the surgery and all was well.

Paula said, "I don't think I would have gotten on the table for that surgery had Dad not come through and said it would all be okay."

Sometimes Spirit will disclose a secret. Paula's dad showed us him holding a granddaughter on the Other Side. Paula only has grandsons. We asked who had a miscarriage? Faith began to cry! She had never told her mom about the miscarriage. That moment changed a lot between Faith and Paula's relationship for the better. They are much closer now. We encouraged them to do something in memory of Faith's baby girl.

When Paula's husband first spoke to her, he was a little skeptical about the reading, but he said if she thought it would help he was all for it. She asked if he wanted her to tell her dad anything? He said, "No, but just in case this is real, tell your dad to tell my mom 'Hi.'" Paula's dad came through at the reading and said it was already done. Paula went home and told her husband and he couldn't wait to tell their pastor.

After Paula and Faith left the reading, they had to stop at the drugstore. Christmas music was playing and then Paula said, "Faith, do you hear that song?" It was a song that was played at Paula's wedding, which is not a Christmas song. After it played, it went back to Christmas music. Her dad was still at it, bringing through more signs.

Paula says Lacey and I saved her life, but the truth is her dad saved her life. We just got to be the lucky ones to deliver the healing messages. When I spoke with Paula that day at the nail table, she was so happy and had a spark of light back in her eyes!

We did another reading for Paula and Faith in September, 2018. I looked at her and said, "Paula?" For a split second I wasn't sure if it was her because there was no spark in her eyes: only heaviness, emptiness, and sadness.

Another suicide. Her son Christopher died one year ago. This was a very personal reading. It is always so heart wrenching to read for a parent who has lost a child.

One Sunday before church, Paula asked her husband, "What's wrong with my mouth?" He told her it was fine. When they got to church, someone asked her what was wrong with her mouth and then another friend noticed it and they thought she was having a stroke. They took her to the local hospital and they transferred her to a larger hospital. Faith was with her and called her brother Christopher and he beat them to the hospital. After they admitted Paula and she was doing better, Chris went on home that night. Faith got the call the next day that her brother had committed suicide.

Chris came through at the reading with so much love for his family. Lacey told them, "I have never seen this before, but Chris is kneeling before you and telling you he is sorry." That's all Paula needed to hear!

To lose not only one, but two, people you love dearly to suicide is beyond imaginable. Paula feels she has a purpose to help others who have lost loved ones to suicide. She has been able to find healing and peace through the readings to know they are okay and still with her.

She asks that when someone loses a loved one to suicide, not to judge them or say where their Soul has gone. Just hug them, love them, support them, and say nothing at all. It is through our "small acts of kindness" that we are able to help others heal.

After the first reading, Paula took what we said and honored her granddaughter's Soul. Faith stopped by the house one day and Paula asked her to come outside with her. She had planted a flower garden with all pink flowers and a sleeping Angel statue. She had placed a cross that she saw had the word "Hope" on it in the garden. Faith had said if she had a baby girl she was going to name her "Hope Elizabeth."

Susan's Story

As we sat down to write Susan's story, I asked her what sparked her to get a reading. She said she had read our story on our website some time ago. One night she had a dream and Leo was in it. She knew of Leo because her oldest daughter was two classes behind him in school and, of course, the pizza place.

Susan was surprised when she had this dream in the Fall of 2014. She messaged Lacey to help her interpret it. In the dream, Leo was telling Susan she was taking the wrong street. She saw many streets and she was headed down one of them when he spoke to her. Lacey helped Susan understand and interpret the dream. She simply needs to take another path in life.

Susan said she met her husband July 5, 2002, and it felt like they had known each other for years. In mid 2003, Susan and her husband found out that she was pregnant with their first child together. Susan's due date was in February, 2004. One day, as her husband was painting a room in the house, Susan was watching a movie about a boy in high school who was diagnosed with leukemia. Susan was in tears as she watched the movie. It really affected her!

During her pregnancy, Susan dealt with gestational diabetes and had to administer shots to herself. On January 26, she went to her regularly scheduled appointment. After seeing the doctor, he sent her home to pack a bag to prepare for a c-section delivery that night.

Everything happens for a reason. On March 4, her husband was diagnosed with the same cancer/leukemia as the boy in the movie. If Susan would have had their baby on her due date, her husband wouldn't have been there because of being sick.

On the morning of February 3, 2005, Susan dropped her oldest daughter off at school and took her youngest to her mom's house. She then took her husband to his doctor's appointment. Little did they know that he would be sent to another hospital to the transplant floor for a blood transfusion. His oxygen levels were very low and his numbers didn't look good.

Upon arriving at the hospital that day, her husband told them that if they had to put him on a ventilator he wouldn't come off of, he didn't want that. He had been on a ventilator before for nine days and he was firm on his decision.

The nurses always commented on what a good patient he was. He wasn't a complainer at all, but things were different that day. He was agitated by the oxygen mask and feeling really bad.

While there that day, their pastor who had married them and also baptized him and their daughter happened to be in the area. Their pastor stopped by to see them and while he was there, he renewed Matt and Susan's marriage vows.

Susan asked her husband if he wanted her to call his family and he said no! He later became noncoherent. Susan asked the staff to shut the view of the monitors off in his room. He passed four hours later on February 4, 2005.

When Susan came to us for a reading in 2018, she was nervous and skeptical. She wondered if we made it up. What she knew was we didn't know her story. Lacey and I prefer it when we know nothing about the person we are reading for because Spirit brings it in such a way that the skepticism is dissolved.

As we sat down, Lacey cleared the energy in the room. Immediately I felt Susan's stress. I told her, "You have been carrying and dealing with this huge load for a while." Spirit showed it to me like a huge wooden yoke that oxen carry. Barely able to carry it, they kept emphasizing the burden of this load.

Then Spirit showed me two eights. Susan said she is the youngest of eight children and later she remembered that her birthday is on the eighth. Lacey connected with her grandparents. Even if our loved ones have passed before our birth or we didn't know them, they still know us! Lacey talked about a favorite car or vehicle her husband had. Susan said he had a favorite truck.

Spirit showed me her husband trying to lift the yoke of burden from her that she had carried for 13 years. He wanted to thank her for carrying out his last wishes. Her husband told her it was his decision, and he took responsibility for his final wishes. After the reading, Susan felt lighter because he took the load off of her and is taking responsibility for the decision that was life changing.

She went to the cemetery a week after the reading to have a conversation with him. This was a time of thanking him for taking her load. Spirit never fails to heal our Souls!

Sharon's Story

Where do I begin? The day my dad was diagnosed with lung cancer was devastating. How could this be? He had a five-bypass surgery at age 49. He survived two heart attacks and a stroke. I couldn't think about life without my dad in it. He was the only man I could depend on until I met my husband. He was my dad, the strongest man I knew. He was always there for me. He always had the answer. He taught me how to ride a horse and showed me what a good horse was. We talked about bloodlines. He liked cutting horses and I liked pleasure horses, although we both appreciated a good horse.

Over the next few months, Dad went through chemo and radiation. The doctor said his cancer was treatable. There were so many people praying for him that death was not an option. Then in January, he was told there was nothing more they could do. My dad called me that night and told me he was dying and had lived a good life. I was devastated. After he hung up, all I could do was cry. My husband and I were living in a camper at the time as our house was being built and I could feel the walls closing in. I couldn't imagine life without him.

I took a leave of absence from work and helped take care of my dad. I wanted to spend every minute I could with him, as well as help my mom. I also prayed that God would heal him. There were good days and bad days. We didn't talk about him dying. We just took one day at a time. I would go home on Friday, while my siblings would help on the weekends. I was exhausted and needed a break, but also felt guilty leaving. I didn't cry in front of my dad, but cried all the way home. It was so hard watching him go downhill. My dad always told us to never put him on life support. He was very adamant about it. He was also a very strong man and seeing him deteriorate was killing me. I knew Dad didn't want to live like that. I found myself praying that God would take him. I couldn't take seeing him in so much pain. All I really wanted was for my dad to be okay.

I went home the last Friday night. I got a call from my sister on Sunday morning. The call was odd as I could hear a whisper of my name before Shelly started talking. She asked if I was coming over. I asked her if I needed to. She said Dad wasn't doing very well. She also told me not to drive crazy. I got in my car and headed to my parents' house. I was driving fast. As I drove, there was an eagle standing in a field close to the road. As I passed the eagle, it turned its head toward me. I called my sister and asked if Dad was still alive. She told me he was. When I arrived at my parents' house, there were lots of cars. I knew it wasn't good. I went inside and my family was standing around his bed. My mom sat beside him holding his hand. I just knelt down beside him and said, "Oh, Dad." Seconds after that, he took his last breath. That was the worst day of my life.

Life just wasn't the same after losing my dad. I cried every day on the way to or from work and then at home. I was so sad. Everyone around your life goes on and I was just trying to make it through today. I wanted to call him and hear his voice saying, "Sharon Sue," but knew that was never again going to happen.

And then one day my life changed. I went to get my hair done by my cousin Cheryl. She has been my beautician since she was in beauty school. I sat down in her chair as I always did. She began telling me that my dad was proud of me. I know I looked at her with a puzzled look. She then told me he was proud that I was carrying on his legacy through my dogs. I asked her why she said that. What I had not told anyone, including my husband, was that I had been naming my new pups in his honor. I would think of names that reminded me of Dad.

How could Cheryl know this? She proceeded to tell me she was a Medium. I always watched "Sylvia Browne" and wondered if this was true and now my cousin just delivered a message that changed my life. I sat in her chair and the tears flowed down my cheeks. I no longer felt the emptiness I had felt for the last year. I was able to smile again and remember the happy times with my dad. My dad doesn't always come through when I'm at Cheryl's shop, but when he does, we laugh. I remember one day there was a song that came on the radio that Cheryl felt she needed to hear. The lyrics were "I'm a Cowboy." We both laughed as we knew it was Dad as I always referred to him as a cowboy.

I'm so thankful to my cousin Cheryl for the gift that she was given as she can bring joy to so many people, including myself. Love ya Cuz!

On another occasion, I was having issues with my car. The anti-lock light was on. I had gone to Quincy and when I got home, I noticed the light was off. I then began my chores of feeding the dogs. I had just come from the barn and went to the garage to get dog food. There was music playing that was the same as what was playing in the barn. My car radio was playing. I opened and closed the door and it quit. I then went behind the garage and fed my dogs. When I put my bucket of food away in the garage, the radio was playing again. This time I opened the door, took the key out of the ignition, and closed the door and the radio quit. I called my husband and asked him to check my car when he came home and, sure enough, the radio was playing. The next morning, I went to start my car and the battery was dead. I had to call our mechanic to come get it as it had to be jump started. They left it in their shop over the weekend and on Monday morning, it started right up. Shortly after that, the burner stopped working on our electric glass top stove. Something just didn't feel right, so I messaged Cheryl and asked if there was anything I should be concerned about. She told me she saw a warning sign. I had just begun selling real estate and wasn't real comfortable going into empty houses with people I didn't know.

There was another time I had an issue with my stove. It just started beeping and wouldn't stop. My husband had to turn off the breaker in order to get it to stop. He asked if he needed to call Childers to have it looked at. I just laughed and told him no, as I knew it was my dad. I again messaged Cheryl and asked if I should be concerned. I told her I was driving up north to meet someone whom I was delivering a puppy to. Cheryl told me it was a good fit. That made me feel good as I felt it was going to be a great home. I have since sent her another puppy and made a lifelong friend.

Just yesterday on Thanksgiving, my husband had me read something on Facebook called "The Empty Chair." As I read, tears started to flow as I was missing my dad. Later that day, I baked a pie. I shut the oven off and didn't notice until later that the light didn't shut off. I pressed the button three to four times, but it still wouldn't shut off. As we started to leave for Thanksgiving at my mother-in-law's, my husband realized the kitchen light was on. He went back inside and turned it off. He told me the oven light was on, so he shut it off. I asked if he got it to shut off, as I tried three to four times and he said, yes. I laughed and told him it was obviously my dad and not his then. We had a nice talk on the way to town about our dads whom we miss dearly.

Electronics and eagles aren't the only things that make me aware my dad is around. I was at work on my dad's birthday. I was struggling because he was on my mind. When I got to my office after lunch, I looked up and my peace lily had bloomed. I fought the tears and left for the day. There was another time that this happened and it was when I returned to work after my Aunt Sandy's funeral. She was like a second mom. I cried for over six months after she passed away. Every time Alan Jackson's song "Sissy's Song" came on the radio, I cried as it reminded me of my Aunt Sandy. Needless to say, one of my Aussies is named after this song.

—Sharon

Cheryl's Reflections . . .

I loved my Uncle Jerry and I love when he comes through with a tidbit for my cousin Sharon! He has also had me deliver messages to her sisters Shelly and Connie, as I do their hair, too. I have to laugh because the first time this happened for all of them, the look on their faces was priceless. To know Uncle Jerry is also priceless. I see his boyish charm come through and all of his mannerisms. He always makes me smile, but as I read Sharon's story, I cried for several minutes. He has brought healing for his family through me and I will never forget Sharon telling me, "Dad always liked you!" I love you Uncle Jerry and keep those messages coming because as you well know, they have brought much healing. I now get to see Sharon smile (most of the time) instead of cry when we talk about her dad. It's truly a blessing for all of us.

Chapter 9

HEAVENLY CONNECTIONS

Archangels

I'm not sure why but I have seven Archangels helping me. For the most part, what I have read is that we have two Guardian Angels. So when I had seven show up and they are all Archangels, I was surprised, to say the least. I just figured it's one of two things: either I am a hot mess and need a lot of help or I have become a rule breaker. This really bothered me for a long time because of everything I've read. I finally decided, what's the big deal, just roll with it.

As Lacey and I do readings, I realize they all are here to help us with our readings so, in essence, they are here for everyone we read for. When I first started to study and take classes, I was drawn to the Angels in general. I thought I would learn all the details of each Angel. For some reason, I just can't seem to remember it all so I just let them take care of whom I need for what purpose.

If I need to direct someone in a certain direction, I let them guide me and sometimes that guidance is to look up their information and pass it on.

Don't get too hung up on being an expert on one certain thing. In my case, just when I think I have it figured out, they throw me a curve ball.

Be open to growth and change and be ready to shift when necessary. All of our experiences are different and they are all important. Be unique in what you do. Customize it as Spirit guides you. It all seems to work out!

Archangel Michael

You know how it is when you have a lot of family or friends who you are close to, but there is that one who you are especially close to. You have no idea why, but you have a special bond with them. That's how it is with me and Michael. I wasn't raised in a church that focused on him. Of course, I knew he was God's greatest warrior, if you will. I can remember feeling something different in me when we would read about him. I guess I'll have to wait until I cross over to the Other Side to fully understand our connection.

Michael means "He who is like God." I see him as a strong, fierce warrior for good. He protects me at all costs. I can completely count on his bravery and strength, but most of all, his love. He teaches me all of this and more. It is a chapter in my life that is continually being written.

I was told one time that maybe we called on Archangel Michael too much. I gave it a second thought, paused, and then said, "Nope, he'll let me know if that's the case." He can always delegate my situations out if he wants, but he is my "Go To!" Really, I think he would be hurt if I didn't call on him: my Light, my Protector with his Sword of Truth. For me, he sits at the head of my Archangels. They are all so important as is he, but someone has to lead, so lead on Michael.

Seven Archangels

Archangel Raphael

Raphael is the "healer." His name means "God heals." When we have physical issues, we call on him. I grew up with horses and when

Ben and I had kids, we gave them horses for 4H projects. They started with a pony and then as they outgrew him, they each got a horse. We would put out a round bale of hay for them to eat. One very wet Spring we noticed my son's horse was coughing. I called my older brother and dad to come look at his horse. They inspected the horse and looked at the hay. The hay had molded so it caused the horse to have what they call "the heaves." This is a lung disease causing airway obstruction. At that time, there wasn't anything that could cure it. I prayed to Archangel Raphael and the horse got better, and I never noticed any more symptoms. I was floored to say the least!

I never told anyone but Ben this story that I can recall. I was so upset that we had done this to our son's horse and I felt enormous guilt. Archangel Raphael answered my prayers. I sobbed uncontrollably that day. I was still a bit skeptical, but the labored breathing never returned.

Call it what you will—a miracle, a healing—or if you can't believe it, I get that too. All I know is my personal experience to be true! I prayed to Archangel Raphael and he wrapped his healing wings around this horse and healed him for me. Yes, he did it for me because I asked. How powerful and beautiful is that? I carried so much shame and guilt so he took care of the horse and me!

Archangel Uriel

He sheds light on situations. If you pay attention, he can give you a heads up on upcoming obstacles. If you lost something and it appears out of what seems like thin air, it just might be him.

Archangel Ariel

Has a very sweet, calm energy that I feel from her. I feel her most in nature. I love the outdoors and this is where we connect on a deeper level.

Archangel Haniel

Is very connected to astrology. I think it is interesting how much different moon changes affect our lives. She helps us to stay centered as we move through life.

Archangel Jophiel

She helps us see the beauty in all. She has helped me to always see the good in people. When I asked for an Angel to help me write this book, I feel she has done that.

Archangel Metatron

He and his brother Sandalphon are the only Archangels known to have been human. I feel our strong connection because he understands the human aspect of me. He helps me organize and he helps me write. He gets me!

Keep in mind that I am NOT an expert on Angels and I have to refer to different books to see which Angel to call on for certain situations. As I said before, don't get hung up on being an expert. Just call out for the perfect Angel for your situation. They know who they are and they will come running.

Spirit Guides

Chief Two Trees

Now granted, maybe the name is right or maybe not, but this is what he allows me to call him. He is the head of my Spirit Guides. Our past connection brought us together. In some ways, it is as if I am he on some mystical level. He is strong, quiet, and a fierce leader. I'm in awe in his presence. I met Chief Two Trees when I did the

Medicine Place CD of Raymon Grace. At first, you just think you are making things up, but each time I have done this exercise, he was always there. I am humbled and honored that he chose me to work with. His wisdom will stop you in your tracks. He gathers the others around a circle as they sit together like family. He is my ringleader: my Chief.

Running Water

Beautiful and young, she sits by Chief Two Trees' side. She, too, is wise for her age and quiet. It's interesting because I'm not so quiet. I pray they rub off on me. She is the female Energy that completes Chief Two Trees. They work as a team for me and she is learning as she serves as one of my Guides. It's interesting because we are all climbing the Enlightenment Staircase, so I am honored to do my part here on earth as they advance on the Other Side. We are like a tribe that works together and we take care of each other. Again, I am humbled.

Jasper

When I started studying and paying attention to signs, I was surprised at how many times the name Jasper came up. I don't think Jasper is a very common name—at least not in our neck of the woods. I would see it on a license plate, in a store, or hear it on the radio, but the one that finally made me realize that he was one of my Spirit Guides was when I saw it on a billboard. I laughed out loud when I saw it and said, "Yep, I get it now!" Glad it wasn't on a sledge hammer. Jasper is very sweet and kind. He has a quiet calmness about him that speaks volumes. He helps me stay calm and to step back and really look at what is going on in a situation. He is wise and very patient, which is a virtue he tries to help me with!

Calvin

Wow! I wish you could see Calvin. He is a tall black guy with flaming red hair—and I mean red hair like a fire hydrant! He is a smartass, to say the least, and he loves aggravating me at every turn. My grandson Malik could see Spirits in 3D form when he was younger and he would tell me that this guy was with me all the time. At first, I thought he was one of my Guardian Angels, but I got to know him and I realized he is one of my Spirit Guides. Now he loves to tease and influence me at every turn. It's like poking a stick at a snake to see if it will strike. I love Calvin because he reminds me not to take life so seriously! We must remember to laugh and have some fun while we are here and, apparently, when we cross over, too.

Leo

I was surprised when Leo showed up as one of my Spirit Guides. I have always read that people you know or family members are NOT your Spirit Guides. I guess if that's the case, he is a rule breaker (in a good way). I think because of the fact that he led Lacey and me out into the public forum, it is his job to see it through. I think he knew we would never have stepped forward if he would have just set back and waited, so he gave us a not-so-gentle push over the cliff. It's his kind-heartedness and perseverance to help others that landed him this gig. He is not easy to turn down. His American/Italian charm gets me every time!

Albert

When I opened my business, Raymon told me to invite in a lawyer from the Spirit World. Of course, I asked for the best and along came Albert. He is a small, partially bald man who wears round, wire-framed glasses and a brown tweed suit. He is quiet in nature and very good at his job. He's always prepared when I call on him. He has saved me many times. I'm thankful he is on my side!

Yogagee

Before I teach yoga class, I connect with my Yogagee. I met him during a Reiki session that my older sister was doing on me. During the session, he just popped in and showed himself to me. There he was seated crosslegged in front of me. He is of Eastern Indian decent. I asked him for guidance before each class I teach. I know when something out of the blue comes up for me to add to the class: it's he. I go into class with an agenda, but when I connect to him it usually changes for the better. He is deeply rooted in the traditional, authentic teachings of his roots. I am a better yoga teacher because of him.

Spirit Guide Legend

The one and only! What a legend of a man he was in the world of entertainment! This part of life will make you say she surely doesn't think she connected with his Spirit.

When I started taking classes from my friend Raymon Grace, who taught me how to dowse, he also taught me how to help cross over those Spirits that are stuck and earthbound. Legend was one of those Spirits. When, at every turn, I was seeing his memorabilia everywhere, hearing his songs on the radio stations that don't normally play them, and stumbling across Legend-related things at every turn, I finally realized he was knocking on my door.

Now, who am I to be connecting with such a famous Spirit? I pushed it away, pushed around it, past it, until I was exhausted at trying to avoid him.

As I am telling you this, I am even laughing and thinking how crazy this sounds. Crazy as it might sound, it's true! I finally answered the call. He came to me to see if I could help him cross over.

I didn't have confidence in myself in helping him. Really, who did I think I was to help the one and only Legend? He was insistent that I put the skills to work that Raymon had taught me to help Souls cross over.

I took him down the path that was beautiful and calm and to the limestone steps, but couldn't quite get him to cross. I asked a friend who was more accomplished at this than I so she brought his mother forward to help him—and he crossed easily! I didn't care who helped him, just that he made it to the Other Side.

Here is the process I use to help Spirits that are earthbound to cross over. As in Legend's case, he was stuck here because of all his fans. He was and still is so loved and he was so famous and successful that it's hard to leave here. The pull was so strong for him to stay because we wanted it and he lived and breathed his fans.

I asked him if he wanted help to cross over to the Other Side and he said he did, but yet, was hesitant. I explained that once he crossed over, he would have so many more ways of connecting and helping others here. Keep in mind, I was new at this at that time.

I closed my eyes and relaxed and created a beautiful path to walk down: rolling hills, grass, flowers, and specific trees to touch, smell, and feel the experience. We walked over a bridge with a beautiful creek flowing under it. We made it to these ten large limestone steps. As we walked, I talked about all the beautiful and amazing Spirits that are there to help us on our journey. God, Jesus, and the Angels to name a few, but the important thing that I learned after I failed to completely finish the job—he was a momma's boy! When she was asked to come forward to help him, he went immediately. Family or those whom we were close to while we were on earth are important to bring forward and help with the process.

I have since gotten more personal with those who come to me for help and it works very well.

Was it Legend and did I help with the process, or was he one of my catalysts that showed up in my life to help me gain confidence and practice helping Souls cross over? To me, it doesn't matter. What does matter is I am now sure I do help those Souls cross over. Many times, they set the scene and the approach we use, and I gladly oblige.

Cathy's Story

One of my first readings I did was for my friend Cathy. I asked Cathy if she had someone who had crossed over that was a real Elvis fan. She couldn't think of anyone, but I said I see blue suede shoes and that is why I was thinking Elvis fan. Then I heard the name Emmy Lou Harris, a bluegrass artist. I saw her with a guitar and Cathy said, "Uncle Bob." He was in a bluegrass band back in the day. That was super exciting for both of us. The details were precise for my first reading. Cathy feels like he came through to help me with this process.

Then another time, Uncle Carl came through for Cathy. He showed me the Pearl Harbor bombing. He was in WWII, he had malaria, and it all came through. I didn't know who was the most surprised, me or Cathy. She feels like he came through to help her give a message to his daughter.

Cathy and I have been friends since I opened my business in Jacksonville in 2006. When I realized that I might be a Medium—and I emphasize "might"—she said one night, "Why don't you read me?" and this was the result. Who knew the journey had begun?!

Cathy asked at one reading if I could tell her the name of her Spirit Guide. So I sat with it and I went through a couple of names, but it just wasn't feeling right. Then Geronimo came up. Yes, that was it. He showed me himself as a dark-skinned, handsome man of Mediterranean descent—so I thought. The next day as I was driving into town, a song came on the radio. It was "Geronimo." Confirmation sent!

Cathy and I went to see our friend Deb, who is a Medium, for a reading. She saw a strong connection to Native Americans. Cathy was lost for a moment, which often happens during a reading. I call it "reading amnesia." Sometimes the most obvious message that we receive is one we just can't seem to grasp. Then it hit her! Cathy's given name is Winona, which means "first daughter," and it is an Indian name. Hence the connection!

After the reading as we were driving home, Geronimo showed himself to her. He showed himself younger with short hair in a button-down shirt. Cathy went to bed late that night and he appeared again and said, "I am THE Geronimo." He said the reason he came to her in that form was so she wouldn't be afraid.

The next morning as she was driving to work, he came to her and told her to look him up on the internet. So she did and it brought up a picture of him, his wife, and children. He looked exactly the way he had shown himself to her. During her reading with Deb, it came up that she needed to meditate by the fire. Cathy was at her firepit a few days later and he came to her again to let her know that she was actually one of his wives in a past life. She was having a past life experience of giving birth to his child. The other thing that had come through at the reading was Deb felt someone being scalped. Geronimo lost multiple family members in that way. To this day for the rest of this lifetime, Cathy will work with him as her Spirit Guide.

I let my intellectual mind come into play, which taught me a valuable lesson. I thought Geronimo was her Guardian Angel, but he came to her in the reading with Deb as her Spirit Guide. I got his name and dark skin but didn't connect Native American.

Again, I learned a lesson! Trust the process and don't get into your head too much. Just deliver what you get in a reading and Spirit will clear the muddy waters! Guaranteed!

Chapter 10

REFLECTIONS OF THE SOUL

Faith

You have always heard you have to have faith! Funny thing about faith, it comes and goes, or should I say sometimes we have to dig deep to find it.

When we sit down to do a reading, it's nice when people have faith that they will get to hear from their loved ones. But sometimes we get that person who is a skeptic. I really get excited when they come in and they don't have a drop of faith in the whole process because we have seen it happen time and time again: Spirit will rock their world.

Sometimes the messages are coming through like rapid fire. Trust me. They leave with faith and trust in the process. It doesn't get much better than that!

Michelle's Story

As a child I remember being scared of my grandma. My family was never affectionate. It wasn't until my freshman year in high school when my grandpa passed that I told my grandma for the first time I loved her. She did not say it back; she gave me a very blank look, which made me even more afraid of her.

It was surprising then that for the rest of my high school athletic career, she would come to most of my games and track meets. We gradually started to become friends. After I graduated high school, it became a priority for me to know my grandma.

I went to her house every day for hours at a time—most days it was all day. We looked through old pictures, she told me about her childhood, and we laughed a lot. We eventually became best friends. Every time I left her house, she hugged me and told me she loved me.

When I left for college, I called two to three times a week. When I would come home for holidays and summer breaks, I spent all of my time with her. When I moved back home, I took her to doctors' appointments and we went for dinner most nights. As she got older, she spent more time in the hospital. When I went to visit, we would still laugh and carry on. She seemed to feel better when I was there.

Then one day I got a call at work and was told to get to the hospital as soon as possible. All of my family, except my brother and myself, were already there. Less than ten minutes after we got there, she passed. I knew the rest of the family was upset, but I was devastated. I had just lost my best friend.

The next several weeks were a blur. I felt lost. All of a sudden, my life spiraled out of control. I started to drink heavily, I was a mess, and this went on for about two years.

One day I woke up and decided to make a change. With some help from my friends, I quit drinking and started to exercise daily. When I ran, I felt some kind of presence with me. I really thought it was the Spirit of my high school track coach. It was strong enough that I could not ignore whatever it was.

So I went to Cheryl for a private reading. She told me things about my life she would have no way of knowing. She told me my grandma was with me all the time. When I was running, it wasn't my coach talking, it was she. She was riding a motorcycle with her dog alongside me. I rode motorcycles at her house as a child. Cheryl even told me the color.

For an hour I heard everything Cheryl said to me, but the most important part was my grandma was okay and by my side every day. After my reading, I felt a significant shift inside me. I felt loved in a way that, in turn, allowed me to love others even better. I felt a sense of protection with me. That day changed my life.

I had the courage to leave a secure job to jump into a field that I knew nothing about. I would never have had the courage to do that without the reading. It gave me the courage and guidance to turn the corner. Now I'm not afraid to keep turning the corner.

—Michelle

Cheryl's Reflections . . .

As a Medium, I never know what Spirit is going to bring through in a reading. The things I think are significant might not be the piece that is the game changer to heal my client's heart. It's a good thing that Spirit is in the driver's seat or this time, on a motorcycle! Spirit is changing lives one reading at a time!

Debbie S's Story

I discovered Cheryl and Lacey by accident.

I had just recently moved to Jacksonville, and Cheryl's shop was doing a food drive for the community around Christmas. I had been looking for a place to get a massage so I gave them a call. Kill two birds with one stone: massage and help the community. I was scheduled with one of their massage therapists and really liked her so I kept going back. I think it was either the third or fourth time of going that she had told me about Cheryl and Lacey doing readings and I should give it a try. Since there was a group reading coming up soon, I figured why not? What do I have to lose?

I was the BIGGEST skeptic going to this reading. I usually wear my "Gold Star" necklace and poker run sweatshirt, but on this day, my necklace was hidden and I wore nothing that had my son's name on it. Like I said, I was skeptical. Also, my granddaughter's best friend's mom (Julie) happened to show up, coming several miles. Coincidence? I think not now.

So Julie and I are just sitting there listening and kind of giving each other looks, like "okay." Then Cheryl turns to me and says, "You need to come up to the table." I go up and it takes them 30 seconds to convince me that my son was there and telling me stuff there was no way either of them could have known.

Since that first session, I've been able to attend several readings—private and group. I was at a loss after I had lost my son in Iraq. I was one of those people who was very social, loved to party, etc. Afterwards, it was like I had hit a brick wall and it was all I could do to put one foot in front of the other. So when my oldest son recently passed with cancer, I got ahold of Cheryl to get in for a reading.

I have had professional counseling to deal with the deaths of my sons, but Cheryl and Lacey have helped me more than any counseling ever did. As mothers, we just want to make sure that our children are okay and that my boys are together, safe, and watching over me and my family. I have also been able to open up my eyes, heart, and Soul to see the signs that the boys send me.

Thank you, Cheryl and Lacey, for what you do and the help you have given me and my granddaughter Lilly and so many others struggling with the death of a loved one! Also, I'm sorry for all the sleepless nights that Jeremy puts you through because either I or Lilly aren't listening like he thinks we should. We love you!

—Debbie S

Debbie's Granddaughter's Story

I was young when my father passed away. Cheryl and Lacey have helped me in a way nobody else could have. They have let me commu-

nicate with my father and also my grandma who passed a few years ago. They are amazing people with an amazing gift.

—Lillian C (Lilly)

Lacey and Cheryl's Reflections . . .

We believe it was only our second group reading when we first met Debbie. We had about 30-40 people that day and we had just began to publicly offer our readings a couple of months earlier. We can remember Debbie walking through the door and the energy coming off of her was not that of a happy person. At the time, we thought that she didn't want to be there or didn't believe in any of this. We have zero problem with skeptics! Spirit will either protect us completely and avoid the situation or they come through like a lightning bolt with undeniable proof!

As the group reading went on, we honestly didn't even want to venture to that area of the room due to the upset energy she was projecting. But Spirit decided it was time to send that lightning bolt.

We don't remember most things from readings because it's not ours to retain, but every now and again a piece or two just won't leave us!

We remember her son coming through with such precise detailed messages that it COMPLETELY changed her. After the group reading, she contacted us for a private reading. The person who walked in our door for the private reading was NOT the same person who walked into that group reading that day. Gone was the black cloud and anger. She was lighter and had found some happiness again. Words can't describe what her son did for her that day. His messages completely changed her in the best possible way.

After Debbie had her reading, she decided to bring her granddaughter Lilly in so she could connect and we could bring healing messages to Lilly from her daddy. He didn't fail her. He came through with flying colors. We were honored to deliver those healing messages to her!

Jen's Story

I went to my first reading at Inner Harmony about six years ago. This was before I knew Lacey and Cheryl and long before I worked at Inner Harmony. I don't remember how I heard about the reading. I just remember thinking, "Who can I ask to go with me?" I was hesitant to ask most people to go because of the "stigma" that I assumed would follow. Deep down, I was also afraid of who or what might come through. I have always been fairly quiet about my beliefs and experiences. I was intrigued by the idea of attending a reading. I was hoping to hear from my aunt whom I was close to. I have always felt her presence and wanted confirmation that she was truly near me. Well, let me tell you, YOUR idea of what you need and Spirit's idea of what you need are likely vastly different.

My mom and I arrived at the reading and I was nervous. We sat at a table with a couple who looked just as unsure as I felt. Lacey and Cheryl began by telling their story and I was mesmerized. I was hearing them say things that I had felt since I could remember, but never voiced. I was a tangle of emotions while listening to all the messages being delivered that day. I was keeping it all bottled up, of course. That's what I do. I was anxious. I wanted to hear from my aunt. I couldn't imagine why she wouldn't be coming through with something . . . anything.

Then it happened. Lacey motioned to our table and said, "Who here has lost a child?" I froze. I remember thinking, "Someone else please speak up. She CANNOT be talking to me." Nobody said a word. I halfway raised a finger to indicate I had, secretly hoping she wouldn't see it and move on. She was looking right at me and said, "I had a feeling it was you." Okay, that's going to be the end of this, right? We must move on to another subject because I don't talk about this, let alone acknowledge it in front of strangers. She wasn't done. She asked if I talk about it. NO. She asked if I have done anything to honor their memory. No. Then she got to the core of it. She asked, "Do you feel like a mother? I am getting that you don't feel like a mother, but you are." The tears answered before I could. She hit the nail on the head. I didn't feel worthy of the title. I had miscarried TWO babies, would never have a living child to call me Mommy, and I felt like it was my fault. Cheryl then asked if I knew the sex of the baby. After answering I didn't know, she said, "I see a little girl. I show her putting a string of daisies around your neck as she left you. She knew she would have to leave you when she signed up to be your baby on the Other Side. There was a lesson in it for both of you." Wow! Have you ever tried to silently ugly cry? It is so hard. I couldn't speak, I could only nod. Lacey then explained how I needed to do something to honor her memory. Something as simple as lighting a candle or planting a flower or tree. I just needed to do something to acknowledge the loss and start to live.

She was right. Doubtingly, I started lighting a candle every night while reading. It brought me a sense of peace that I hadn't expected. I had been so afraid of making anyone uncomfortable by talking about my loss that I just shoved it deep down inside with every other emotion. Only after acknowledging the loss did I see the profound sadness and guilt I had been carrying. I saw how it was adversely affecting my life.

I have learned so much about myself and remain a work in progress, but that reading was the nudge I needed to start honoring myself. I am trusting myself and listening to that inner voice. I still get sad at times or have a bad day just like everyone else, but I can find new ways to cope and try not to let it affect every aspect of my life. My aunt never did come through and hasn't in any of the numerous readings I have been to. I must get my stubbornness from her. I take comfort in the "knowingness" that she, and many others, are with me. I am more aware to watch for signs. And every time I see a daisy, it brings a smile to my face.

—Jen

Cheryl and Lacey's Reflections . . .

It warmed our hearts to know that Jen took Spirit's advice and honored her babies by lighting a candle. We wish that we could emphasize the importance of taking Spirit's advice because it can be so healing for the Soul. When we do a reading, we always let the group or the person we are reading for know that we have no way of controlling what Spirit brings through. Spirit always knows exactly what we need to hear and who we need to hear from. It's always the healing piece that we need at that moment in time. We have learned not to expect anything specific from Spirit, because Spirit knows best!

Chapter 11

GIFTS FROM HEAVEN

Judene's Story

Life with Lisa is always an adventure. She has made me laugh and she has made me cry, usually from laughing so hard. I just never know what to expect when I am with her. I have been dragged all over the place and to things that I would have never gone to on my own. And even though I am not as big a fan of Bret Michaels as she is, I still went along and had fun. So when she suggested that we attend a reading at Inner Harmony, I was willing to go. I had no idea what to expect, I just knew I was going with Lisa. She asked me that Sunday afternoon in the car before the reading what I thought was going to happen. I replied that I had no idea and I was keeping an open mind. I was thinking to myself, "You asked me to go and that is why I am here." Since then, we have been to several readings together. Here are our stories.

My life is pretty boring, in my opinion. I was raised on a farm in Central Illinois. I attended church at the local United Methodist Church. I went to high school and college. I returned home to start my life. I have one sister and a very large extended family that all live in the surrounding area. I was exposed to loss and death at an early age. My mother's mom was struck and killed by lightning when she was 43 and my mom was 13. As long as I can remember, we visited the cemetery to place flowers on my grandmother's grave for various occasions. I remember when I was 12, I began to fear that my own mother would die when I was 13. So I started praying to my grandmother that I would not lose my mom. I talked to her a lot that year and again when my mom was 43. During that time, I developed a connection with my grandmother, a person whom I had never met and one whom my own mom did not talk about much. I thought I was just praying. I now believe that her Spirit was giving me comfort. I never told my mom my fears. It was not until much later in life that my mom and I talked about it. Ironically, she had the same fears as I. She thought that when I was 13 or when she was 43, she would die. I am sure that she felt her mother as a strong presence in her life as well, even though she was no longer with us.

Growing up on a farm, nature provides many lessons. My father was very in tune to nature and while he did not attend church with his family except at Christmas, he was a believer in a Higher Power. So it should not have surprised me that he would come through during the readings. Over the years, Lisa and I have attended several together and each individually. He usually has a message for me or at least a tidbit so I know that he is there and okay. My dad is one of the subtle ones. He just drops little clues here and there. It took several readings before I claimed the daisies. And then it hit me. When I was growing up, the neighbor lady had a hillside of daisies. We are talking lots and lots of daisies. Driving past her house, my dad and I would have several conversations about Louise and her daisies. I guess it was a fond memory of his. Almost every reading has daisies. Cheryl or Lacey will state that they see a hillside and lots of daisies. With other flowers, there are other stories like someone's garden or at a funeral service. Not mine. It is pretty unique. I have never told them the story of Louise and her daisies. Like I said, it took several times before I realized that the daisies meant my dad. There is a sense of peace when I think of those times in the pickup truck with him and laughing about how many flowers were there and how she had a green thumb.

It is hard to describe the readings unless you have been to one. Each person has his or her own unique experience with them. I always leave there with a sense of healing and a strong sense of peace. The stories that are heard are so powerful. Surprisingly, the readings do not go against my religious beliefs because they actually are in conjunction with the Other Side. Cheryl and Lacey only let light and positive things through. Yes, it can be very emotional and sometimes there is sadness, but there is healing from the Other Side. I have talked to many skeptical people who said that mediums are fake. The naysayers suggest that the mediums googled people or used social media to get info. The skeptics say that the mediums pull information out of you so you become a believer. There is no way that Cheryl and Lacey could have found out all the little pieces of information that were particular to my life and to others in the room. I do use the other services that Cheryl and Lacey provide at Inner Harmony and you are thinking that, well, it is a beauty shop and nail salon so they have access to knowledge that they could use in the readings. We talk a lot about food, current events, and other trivial stuff. It took me a while to remember about the daisies so there is no way that it would have come up in casual conversation.

One of the most powerful readings happened on May 4, 2015. It was a group reading. There were a few tidbits here and there that I knew my dad was present. You are thinking, what tidbits? Well, the daisies. There was a reference to cancer and the person liked to crochet. My mother's cancer had returned and she crochets. There was a reference to fire/smoke. My dad was not a smoker, but he loved to burn brush and ditches. The fire department was called several times when he started burning. During this particular reading, I felt his presence like he was standing right behind me. I had goosebumps. I did not say anything and Cheryl/Lacey commented that he was standing right there. He let me know that he was with my son the day the accident happened and that is why Jimmy was not hurt. Another irony happened on the way to the accident scene. When I was driving to the accident scene, I was literally yelling at my dad asking why he allowed the accident to happen and I felt so mad. I had been shaking for at least 20 minutes after I heard the news that the accident had caused a fatality. After I yelled at my dad, not God, I felt a sudden peace that my son was alive. I heard a voice in my head saying, "He is alive." Call me crazy. I know what I felt and I did not feel alone. Was it my dad's doing or God's? I would say both. I felt a strong feeling of both that day and much love. I needed that closure, not from Cheryl/Lacey, but from my dad.

Another interesting thing is about my mother. I told her about the experience at Inner Harmony. At first, she just listened and nodded her head. I told her about how messages from the Other Side can be sent. Birds and butterflies or electrical issues are fairly common. She wondered about noises. She stated that there is a creak in the hallway. This is how she knew my dad was going to bed—by that creak. After he passed, she would hear the creak and it would scare her because she thought someone was in the house. She later accepted, without my doing, that it was Dad making the noise. It brought her comfort knowing he was here with her. She started looking forward to my trips to Inner Harmony for readings. She would shake her head and agree with me. There were things I would talk about that were said at the readings without making any references to Dad and she would connect the dots. It provided her much comfort as she battled cancer. I should not have been surprised that she would come through after she passed. I felt so much joy from her after she was gone. I missed her greatly, but knew she was in a good place. It warmed my heart that she came through to check on me. She knew what I needed.

The next part is hard for me to share. I told you that Cheryl and Lacey only let positivity and light through. There is no evil or darkness. At one of the last readings, references were made that caused me to think of my grandfather on my mother's side. It bothered me because there was much turmoil and hurt associated with that relationship. As a Christian, I believe in Heaven and Hell. I did not want to believe that my grandfather was in Heaven with my grandmother and mother. At the same time, I did not want to believe that he was in Hell either. He caused my mother so much hurt and anguish. At that reading, memories of him came flooding back that they were making references to him. I did not want to hear from him or feel his presence. I kept thinking it is not him. Then there would be another reference. It is hard to accept that everything is okay on the Other Side when I lived with that hurt and pain that he caused, even though my mother is no longer with me. People talk about the bond between mother and child. However, it goes the other way as well. Children become very protective of their mothers. I am still trying to decipher what it could mean. I know in my head that I need to make peace with the situation, but my heart is not so sure.

On a lighter note, on one of the days I was getting my hair cut and colored, Cheryl stated that she kept seeing a man with a handlebar mustache. She kept asking me if I knew anyone with one. She asked about westerns or actors. I still have no idea what that reference meant. She said it was a strong one. So I am on the lookout for a man with a handlebar mustache. Cheryl did say that if I met such man that he needs to shave that thing off. I still laugh when I think of that story.

No matter what has happened at readings, there is always a sense of peace and healing—if not for me personally, then for the others who are there. I am one of those people who will not own a reference until later. The daisies took me several times to figure out what they meant. I am more aware now. On my son's birthday, there were two cardinals in the yard sitting in the grass. I swear they looked at me. They did not leave for the longest time. Even with the normal noises that would scare them away, they just sat there. There have been so many signs. I find comfort in those. Until you have been and experienced what I have, you may have trouble understanding. I have no doubts.

Lisa has a very strong personality and is full of life. She has her own issues, as we all do. She has had two very strong people come through for her. It is no surprise that her grandfather would be one of them. They had a very strong relationship when he was alive. The other was a person very special in her life who died way too young. It is something that she struggled with for several years before coming to a group session.

—Judene

Lisa's Story

I was intrigued when I found out that there was going to be a group reading held on a Sunday afternoon with two people whom I respected and trusted. I had often wanted to go to readings, but was scared that it would go against my religious beliefs. But when Lacey and Cheryl explained to me that they both believe and that this just reassures that there is more after we pass, I decided that it was an adventure that I wanted to try, but not alone! I asked my friend Judene to go with me. I wanted support just in case. I have to say I was pleasantly surprised. It was such a relaxed, calming, healing place to be. I did not feel uncomfortable at all. In fact, I felt relief, comfort, and forgot about all the problems of the world outside of the room we were all in. As the session began and messages started to come to many in the room, I felt so much healing occurring for the people in the room. I must say that I really did not speak up much because I thought I am sure that is not a message for me. It has to be for someone else. However, when I attended the next group session, a message came through loud and clear that I could not ignore. It was a message from someone who was very special to me. She died way too young. I had met her through work, but we became very close friends, talked every day, shared so many memories—good and bad—with each other, and she was always that person whom I could count on, both professionally and personally, to tell me what I needed to hear, no matter how difficult the truth was to listen to. Sally was one of those people who did not sugar-coat anything, but once she trusted you, she was loyal no matter what. She had your back whether you were present or not! She began a tradition of having a birthday celebration every year. She did not care if I did not want to celebrate it or not, she was going to have a party and I was going to attend! Many years, it was several days of celebration. She did this every year and always made me feel special. She would invite friends and family. One year she even wrote a song for me and had someone sing it for me. It was titled "My Angel," and she wrote the lyrics. They are still in a frame on my wall. On my 40th birthday she really outdid herself. I thought we were meeting with friends and family for dinner and then a celebration. What I did not know is she had gotten with my mom prior and went through family photos and made posters with pictures of each chapter of my life. She had poster-size signs posted in places around town and then to top it off, she had someone dress up to come sing "Happy Birthday" to me. It was something that I would never forget. She was so proud of herself for truly "getting me" on this special birthday! What I did not know at the time was it would be the last party she would have for me. She had medical complications and passed away at the young age of 36. It was eight days before her birthday, for which I had planned a celebration. I literally fell to the floor when I got the call. I had just been on the phone with her the night before, talking almost an hour. We had a song, "Friends," that we would listen to in my office when we needed a pick me up. We had each discussed that when it was our time, we would play that song and give the eulogy for the one we lost. It was a tough day, but I did it for her. I decided from that point forward there would not be any more birthday celebrations because it was too painful. So I guess I should not have been surprised when her message came through loud and clear at the second reading. It started with a saying that she would say with a motion to go with, "Super Star." She said it with attitude and arms in the air. Only people who were around her consistently knew this. It was nothing I had shared, just part of Sally. So when Cheryl said, "I have no idea what this is about, but this is what just came through," and she did the motion, the attitude, and the words. I was stunned! Then Lacey followed by saying she saw a party, balloons, streamers, singing, dancing, etc. I owned it even though I was trying hard not to make eye contact! We then went up to the table to receive even more messages that really hit deep in the Soul. It was about the guilt I was feeling. I had not discussed this with anyone. I had so many feelings of what I missed when I talked to her that night. If I would have been there or stopped by to see her, would I have gotten her to the hospital sooner, etc.? The message was, "There was nothing you could have done so stop trying to figure it out and know I am happy and with my mom." It did not stop there, though. She went on to say the birthday celebrations need to start back up because I am there and miss them. I was crying uncontrollably at this point because all this pressure, stress, and pain were starting to come out. We finished and moved on to others who were in the room, but when I left that night, it was like a black cloud was gone. The healing continued after leaving.

I have become so much more aware of my surroundings from the sessions I have attended. Each time I leave, feeling a sense of calmness, I notice "signs" now that I never did before. For example, when I am having a stressful day or feeling lonely, it never fails I see squirrels or that my friends see squirrels. This was a direct sign of Sally. Usually, there is not just one, but several, sometimes a yard full. One time there was an ear of corn in the yard along with a squirrel holding a nut. I also have noticed dragonflies. When I am at a water park, there is always a dragonfly in the same spot where I sit in the water. It just sits on the rock. Knowing the life expectancy of the dragonfly, we know it is not the same one, but it has never not been there when I am. One of the last times I was there, I was going through a rough patch and this time it followed me from the usual area to the other area I went to and then back to the normal area. So many of these examples have happened. When I was coming home from Chicago, where I had been for work, I noticed a bird on seven of the signs we passed on the interstate.

I said something to the person I was with and she pointed out that it was also on the next five. It was not a hawk, but the same kind of small bird on all twelve signs. My mom often has butterflies and cardinals that she sees and it makes her think of her dad.

In many groups that I attend, small things come through, but one of the last two that I have been to, my grandpa has sent a message. At first it was confusing to me because the messages were more about my grandma who is still alive, but then it made sense because he was always very quiet, shy, and never the center of attention. He was sending them, using her as the reference. They were things he knew I would connect him to. I feel he came through because of issues that my mom was having at the time. It was like he was saying he was there watching over her. My mom was always a Daddy's girl and had a special connection with him. My son and I also had a special bond with him. He was quiet, but you always felt his love, support, and commitment to his family. He was definitely one of the good guys—loyal, dedicated, and hard working. My heart was complete when I knew he was there and watching over all of us, but especially my mom and grandma.

There is one more moment I want to share. After I had knee replacement surgery, I moved into my grandma and grandpa's house because it was one story and I could get around. My mom stayed with me for the first week every night. I kept hearing music that nobody else could hear. At first, I could not recognize what it was, but then I started hearing some of the words. I realized it was one of my mom's favorite songs. I feel like this was Grandpa letting us know he was there. After she stopped staying and I was alone, I started hearing music that was from "Hee Haw" and "Lawrence Welk," which were shows I watched almost every week with my grandma and grandpa when I was growing up. It gave me a sense of calm.

So from my first group reading of not knowing what to expect to the many I have attended, I find myself leaving each one with the same sense of healing and calmness, even when a loved one does not come through for me. It is so wonderful to see people get answers, let go of guilt, forgiveness, etc. I look forward to each and every one that I attend. I am definitely more in tune to my surroundings and signs that are present.

—Lisa

Cheryl and Lacey's Reflections . . .

We are always honored to have Lisa and Judene join our group readings. It's confirmation on our piggyback messages in a group that it brings as much healing as a personal message. A piggyback message in our groups is when Spirit brings one common message that is meant for several in the group. Spirit has a way of delivering as many messages as possible in a short window of time, hence, the piggyback message delivery. We have to laugh as we read Judene's story on the daises because I swear we thought every time daisies come through that we must be stuck on only seeing daisies and just kept repeating it. Good to know it was Spirit and not just us.

As for Lisa and her squirrels, really now as Mediums we want to give as detailed of a reading as possible: you know names, someone has a loved one's special treasure, you know things like that. But squirrels, really?! Even at first as we began this journey of delivering messages, we would hesitate on such a thing as a squirrel nut. Spirit showed us with Lisa that we must deliver the message, no matter how crazy we think it might be!

Whitening Toothpaste

When I was really starting to pay attention to the signs that Spirit was sending me, it was very emotional. I was working in our small hometown of Milton and on my lunch break I drove over to Jacksonville to look for a jacket at a clothing store and to pick up some vitamins.

I ran in for the vitamins and then I drove through the parking lot to the clothing store. On my way over, I was listening to Jewel's CD and one of her songs, "Jesus Loves You," was really standing out to me. There is a line in that song that mentions giving "extra whitening" a try.

I always talk to my Angels when I'm driving. I pulled up to the parking spot and saw a homeless man sitting alone on the bench outside of the store. As I went in, I spoke to him and he glanced at me. He was busy having a conversation with himself or whomever was listening, I guess.

I went in to look for the jacket and couldn't get him off of my mind. I only had $22.00 on me at the time and that was before I had a debit card. I kept praying to see what I should do to help him. I took the twenty dollar bill out of my billfold and folded it over twice. I walked up to him and asked him if he was hungry and he said no. I tried to give him the money, but he insisted he was okay. He was bald on top and the rest of his hair was kind of long and straggly. He smiled at me and only had two or three teeth. As he smiled and walked away, I noticed he had a new box of toothpaste in his jacket pocket and along the side as big as life it said, "Extra Whitening." "There's my sign," I thought as tears rolled down my face.

As I drove away, I realized he wasn't a homeless man. He was an Angel on Earth! I did listen to the Angels that day and I'm the one that got the blessing.

911

Signs are all around us if we just pay attention. Ben had a good friend who was very ill. We were praying for a miracle for him.

I had sent him a book about healing your life. This was the first book that I had read when I started this journey and it was a life changer for me. I asked Ben if it was okay with him if I sent it to his friend and he was good with it.

I had prayed so many times for a healing for him. I was in my van headed to Quincy one day and I was talking to Spirit. I said, "I just need a sign to know that you hear me." I had prayed that his friend would be open to the love and healing prayers we were sending his way.

We all have our own journey and our life path is just that—ours. I think I just needed a sign that God was listening.

I had packaged the book up and was taking it to the post office to mail. As I was having this conversation with God, a police car drove past me on the interstate. All that I saw was 911 on the side of the car. Now keep in mind I had never paid attention to that before. But that day, it was like a neon sign flashing. I was listening to a CD and it kept skipping on the 9th song so I put another CD in and it skipped on the 11th song—so 911 again. Ben's friend was an emergency! When I stopped to mail the package, I looked at his friend's street address and it was 911.

My heart sank as I cried because I knew I got my message.

Chapter 12

A SOUL'S BLUEPRINT

Soul to Soul Connections

That moment when you meet someone and you have an instant connection, you are not sure why, but you open yourself up to them and out comes that inner secret: that story that was never talked about. That incident that has held you captive almost a lifetime.

This happens to me a lot. Really, I think Spirit brings our Souls together and at that moment, that pivotal moment, they either unleash that horrible secret or they don't and they miss the chance for their Soul to heal.

We all have that choice called "Free Will." So you can choose to connect or not. When I met my friend Cathy, I knew immediately that we had a connection. It didn't take long at all for us to become best friends. When you have this connection with someone, know that it is all a part of the blueprint you both laid out while on the Other Side before you came here. We are in what are called "Soul Groups." We came here on a mission to grow our Souls. Different scenarios such as family, friends, business partners, etc. lined up so we could have certain experiences for growth.

Our "Soul Growth" happens much quicker here as humans than it does in Spirit form on the Other Side.

We should all rejoice in the fact that we get to have these experiences, even if they are hard, heartbreaking, unimaginable encounters and events. Just know you are checking off your Soul's Growth list on the Other Side!

Partners in Crime

I was from Pike County and didn't really know too many people in Jacksonville when I opened my business in 2006.

Cathy remembers driving by the backside of my building and was drawn to the deck with a vision of me in the building. As she just told me this, it brought her to uncontrollable tears. What's interesting about this is Cathy and I believe in past lives. In our belief system, we know we made a pact or an arrangement on the Soul level before we incarnated, to meet in this lifetime.

I always giggle when I remember the first time she entered my salon. There she was, 4'10" and bigger than life. She came right up to me and asked if I could dowse on her daughter Rachel's allergies. I was speechless because I still hadn't shared this Energy Work of Dowsing with many. I was afraid that potential and present clients wouldn't be receptive to it and might not come back. I wanted her to talk about it privately. I was shocked, but she was on a mission!

Once I started to open up to the public about our Energy Work and have classes on it, Cathy was one of the first to sign up.

Cathy and I became best friends and attended many classes together through the years. We took several of Raymon Grace's Advanced Dowsing classes together. Boy did we have fun and stories to tell on our road trips. We took Soul Channeling trainings together and many classes on Energy Work.

Cathy is what I call my "Honest Friend!" Now, if I don't want to hear the real truth or if I want a softer, sugar-coated approach, she's not who I call. Truly, I always want the blunt truth and I always call her and she never disappoints.

Cathy always says she felt like she already knew me and I always wanted to connect with her: there comes in the past lives and Soul Group connection. When you have that draw to be with someone or knowingness that you already know them, it's probably because you do. You know them from a past life or they are in your Soul Group from the Other Side.

We started getting together every Tuesday night. I teach a late yoga class that night and an early one the next morning. For the sake of time and a way to save on gas and wear and tear on my vehicle, I would stay the night at my business.

We always work on dowsing. We like to work on us, our businesses, families, and cleaning up the energy of our towns and surrounding areas. We would sometimes do "Soul Channeling" and card readings and, finally, she was my guinea pig on Intuitive Medium Readings.

She's my Ethel and I'm her Lucy! This friendship has evolved and strengthened through the years. She says we have matured. I say the jury might still be out on that one! But truth is we have come a long way and farther yet to go.

We truly are Soul Sisters and we both are so excited to see where our life paths take us together. So if in the future you happen to see a silver camper leaning to one side as it travels down the road, we might be road tripping and gathering a few rocks on the way! To be continued—I love you to the moon and back, Soul Sister!

My Dharma Code

I took my first yoga class in 2002 and I was hooked. After about the third class, our teacher asked if anyone would be interested in taking yoga teacher training. I didn't hesitate for a second—I knew I needed to pursue it. He gave me the names and phone numbers of two yoga studios that offered teacher training. I was drawn to Namasté in Springfield. I had no idea why the yearning was so strong in me to do this. I drove one and a half hours each way three times a week for three years to study yoga and become a certified teacher.

What is clear to me now is it was one of the most important paths for me as being a Medium. I never would have come up with this one on my own so it's a good thing Spirit knows what to do and where to lead us.

I think it was toward the end of my teacher training that I went with my teacher to St. Louis to take a five-day teacher training under Rod Stryker. I had taken different yoga trainings, classes, and workshops under some very wonderful teachers. In January, 2006, I took a five-day silent retreat under Richard Miller that was life changing for me in a way I didn't expect. The amount of healing I received from the many yoga classes at Namasté and abroad holds a special space of healing in me in so many different facets. I was blessed to go to a conference in Colorado where I experienced many different teachers and styles of yoga.

Each class gave me a piece that I needed to reconnect with my Soul. I didn't realize the impact of Soul Growth that I was getting at the time. The lessons and Authentic Traditional Yoga teachings were hard to describe. I only knew that the layers upon layers of all that life had thrown at me was slowly being removed.

I took my first five-day teacher training with Rod Stryker in January, 2005 on "Tantra." It was such a challenge as I was just beginning my yoga path. I was totally drawn to his traditional and, as I explain it, "the full meal deal" of authentic yoga. He took us deep into the traditional path with an enlightened richness. Rod is the teacher that my Soul sought out. Keep in mind, this was just something that I knew I needed to pursue. I never questioned why or for how long or if I was on the right path. I just knew he was the teacher for me and I answered my Soul's call. Sometimes, you just need to step out of the driver's seat and let God take the wheel. I was so excited to learn as much as I could about yoga. Then, in 2006, his training was on "Prana," and in 2007 I dove deep into "Yoga Marma." I wasn't sure where this journey was headed, but my desire was strong. In February, 2008 came "Yoga Sutra." I had taken all of these trainings with my teacher and then in 2009, Rod brought us "The Yoga of Fulfillment," and I took this one on my own. It always amazes me how Spirit works. This was the training that changed my life path! It was meant to be for me to go solo on this adventure.

Yogarupa: Rod Stryker was writing his book, *The Four Desires*, based on this training. If you get the chance to take a class under Yogarupa, you will forever be changed or at least I was. The richness of this class helped me find my Dharma Code: My True Life Purpose!

It was one of my last trainings with Rod on finding our Dharma Code that will forever be etched in my Soul. I had grown and changed in this class and, of course, it came at the perfect time with the perfect teacher to form my path.

Your Dharma Code is your Life Purpose that you and Spirit agreed to on the Other Side: an agreement or arrangement of what you came here to carry out. Never in my wildest dreams did I know that it was to lead me to be an Intuitive Medium.

I can remember doing the steps of working this process out, until I came to my Dharma Code at the training. I remember the shift I felt in my Soul. I didn't know where it would lead me, but I was certain I had uncovered it.

My Dharma Code is "I am a Vessel of Light, on a Voyage of Healing." It was beautifully strange how I never questioned it; I just knew it was real!

This healing is for me and for those whom Spirit sends a message to through me. It just doesn't get much better than that. So be the seeker and don't give up on finding your Dharma Code: Your Life Purpose!

I really thought that I was going to pursue a deeper, extended training with Rod, but after taking this class, it changed the direction of my path. My experience is still moving forward and I took two more weekend Intensive trainings with him. I aspired to take all of Rod's trainings and eventually become a certified teacher under him. But that all shifted after taking the training on "The Yoga of Fulfillment."

My Dharma Code opened me up to my journey of being a Medium. I am and always will be grateful to Rod Stryker for guiding me in a way that has changed my life. I'm glad I took the journey! Yoga will always be a part of my life path and for that I am blessed!

I encourage all of you to be that seeker and follow the path that brings you to your Soul's desire. Commit to never giving up on uncovering your Life Purpose. I suggest whether you do yoga or not, read Rod's book *The Four Desires* and if you can, take a class under him. You will be forever changed as I am!

Spirit has a way of opening the door to your Soul's burning desires. As I studied yoga and did my practice, I was stepping toward Fulfillment. The rich trainings and deep authentic teachings all are a piece to the puzzle of my life.

I'm grateful that I never saw it coming. It came in such an organic form that was untouched by ego. My studies, my practice, and my priceless meditations have all filled my heart's desire. When I chant, I feel Spirit's presence and a joy fills my Soul. I cannot put into words how Rod Stryker's one training and book, *The Four Desires: Creating a Life of Purpose, Happiness, Prosperity and Freedom,* uncovered my hidden jewel! I encourage you to take a look at what Rod has to offer on his website *Parayoga.com* or check out his new app *Sanctuary*.

Dowsing

The easiest way I know how to explain dowsing is through an experience I had as a child. My grandparents were in need of a well for their house. They had a local guy come by and as I observed, he went to the peach tree and cut off a branch that was in the shape of a "Y." He held the two short ends in each hand and as he walked with the long piece out in front of him, I saw the long end of the branch quiver and draw or pull down toward the earth.

As he would walk back and forth, it would draw down in some areas and do nothing in other areas. This process is called "witching for water." When he would walk across a water vein, the branch would engage toward it. This is how they would determine where to drill the well. This process is still used by some today.

This process amazed me as a child. I don't believe in coincidences so the fact that I have taken nine or so Dowsing Classes under my friend and Advanced Dowsing Teacher, Raymon Grace, should not be a big surprise.

I met Raymon Grace in St. Louis back in December, 2002, I think. He was teaching a three-day class on Advanced Dowsing and Emotional Trauma Release. I was nervous and very excited for this training. Raymon is a very no-nonsense, down-to-earth man with a heart of gold. We connected immediately. I was eager to learn his techniques and put them to use.

Through the many classes I have taken from Raymon, I always learned something new. I have always said if you take any kind of class and learn one thing, it is worth your ticket price.

I learned how to clear and cleanup the energy of a person, place, or thing. I encourage you all to check out Raymon's work at *raymon grace.us*. You won't regret it and if you can take a class, it just might change your life like it did mine.

Lacey and I use our dowsing abilities before every reading to clear the people and the space where we are doing the reading. I do my part before the session and she does it at the beginning of the reading. During some readings, I will pick up my pendulum and check on something or clear something. When I'm not quite getting a clear answer from Spirit, I always check and confirm it with dowsing.

Dowsing has been a huge part of my daily life since I met my friend Raymon. When I feel off, I simply stop for a moment and get myself balanced by dowsing.

I am not able to share with you all of the ins and outs of dowsing so that's why I encourage you to check out his website. For me, it is pertinent to be clear and balanced before I do any reading.

This requires me to do a daily—and sometimes more than one—clearing on myself every day.

The hardest part of dowsing for me was to remove myself, so to speak, and get out of my own way, as not to influence the dowsing results.

I am grateful for everything I have learned from Raymon. When I needed assistance or a double check on my work, he would do that. Not many teachers come along in life who make a life-changing impact, but when they do, it can rock your world. He helped guide me down a path that not only helped me help others, but he helped heal my Soul.

I am more confident in my readings to know I have set myself up on a good foundation to work from. Dowsing to clear the space and the people before Lacey and I do a reading is like you cleaning your house to prepare for company.

Energy Work comes in so many different forms and being a Medium, I can see how we are all simply channeling Spirit. We just all use a unique and different approach or tool to get the job done.

Another extremely valuable process that I got from Raymon was when we did "The Medicine Place" in class. He would beat a smooth steady rhythm on a drum as we sat or laid down for this practice. His gentle voice would take us on a healing journey and we got to meet our Spirit Guides. The first time I did this, I felt as if I were making it up, but to this day, the two Native American Guides I met at the Medicine Place are still with me. I am always learning from them and they are invaluable to me as a Medium.

You have to keep learning the technique and keep practicing and pray you find a teacher who is rooted in truth and the good of mankind.

I had no idea that learning to dowse would be one of the modalities that would lead me to be a Medium. Raymon once said, "I had no idea you did that." I replied, "I had no idea, either." He then asked me how it worked. He asked if you had to be present or can it be done long distance. It's like dowsing. You don't have to be present. He asked if he could ask me something and I could tune in and check on it. I was honored to help him. It's always nice to get a chance to give back to your teacher.

Lacey and I use Raymon's work to clear people, but we also use it to clear homes and businesses. We incorporate smudging and crystals and salts to aid in the process.

During our life journey, we need to explore and study as many modalities as we can and then use what works best. For me, dowsing and clearing out negative energy is priceless. Lacey and I are asked many times if we are afraid to channel because it might open a door to negative or dark Spirits. Our answer is always no. Our Angels and Guides always protect us and I have Raymon's work that he taught me. Dowsing and Raymon have been a true blessing on my path.

I thank you and am eternally grateful for all of the lessons I have learned from you, Raymon, and honored to call you friend!

Soul Channeling

The next step on my healing path was a process of a group of people for whom you represent their loved ones. You were picked by them and you allowed that Soul that you represented to come through you.

You would feel their feelings and take on their mannerisms. It was an honor to help in this healing process. Now as I look back, I have to laugh at the fact that I was really channeling Spirit; we all were. I did several years of this process and even got certified as a facilitator at the beginner level.

I was always amazed at how much Spirit could bring through to their family. My friend Cathy, my daughter Lacey, and I would attend these workshops together. I knew this was a healing part of our progress without ego, but I never once thought about it as channeling Spirit.

I think I was aloof to this so it could profoundly impact my process without ego getting in the way. You see, we all have things in our life that need healing and, as that progresses, you are then able to advance toward Enlightenment so you can then help others on a different level.

Each time I represented someone's family member or friend, or someone who impacted their life, I received another piece to my own puzzle. It was so subtle. Spirit works in such a quiet, gentle way that I couldn't even detect it.

So many times as we would go through this process and had the honor to represent someone's loved ones, we would get our own healing. One time, it was Cathy's turn to have the experience. She chose me to represent her mother Fran. Cathy was very close to her mom and never dreamed she would lose her before her own 40th birthday. They had that eternal bond as if they were one. Her mother was only 57 when she passed. Any time we would talk about Fran, she would break down in tears and sometimes couldn't even speak! Not only was I honored to represent her mom, but I was very excited to possibly bring her some peace and closure.

As I represented her mom, Cathy saw her mother's mannerisms come through me. Cathy said, "It's hard to explain, but Cheryl even took on her look." It was glimpses of her mother who had been gone at least 20 years. This process allowed me to channel her loved one.

Keep in mind, we had no idea that we were actually doing a physical reading.

Now I realize how important this part of my work was in relationship to Lacey and I doing intuitive readings.

Spirit finds a way to heal our sadness and helps us move forward. I don't know how many times Cathy and I talk about how amazing this process is. It's as if your loved one just made a personal visit so you can once again reconnect with him or her.

Now when we talk about Cathy's mom Fran, she is so much more peaceful. Even though she misses her, it has eased her pain because Cathy knows her mom is still with her and at peace.

My Visitation Dream

While I was putting the final touches to my book, I had a visitation dream. As I have said before, during these dreams you are actually in them and have a visceral experience.

A young lady came to me and was very upset because I was being devoured and swallowed up by getting stuck. She was on a mission to deliver a message to me. I asked her what her name was and she told me "Devee." I asked her who she was and she explained that she was one of my new Spiritual Guides. I then asked her what level she was and she replied, "Level 6." I then asked what level one of my other Spirit Guides was, she replied, "He's a Level 2." Well, I knew this was very important because if he is a Level 2 and as much as he has helped me, I can't even imagine where she will take me on this "Medium Journey."

I remember driving a car and she was with me. Spiritually she explained to me that I was to drive down this grassy road and not to stop under any circumstances. As I turned on the road, it was a dirt road with grass in the middle and tall grass on the sides of the road: a lot like driving back to a field off the beaten path.

She kept telling me not to stop, just keep going. The road was winding and there was a car off the road on the left. It wasn't running, the lights were off, and it was parked. She was in a panic and kept saying, "Don't stop. Don't stop!" After I passed it, it started up and turned on its lights to follow me! She kept telling me, "Keep going." I drove a little farther and there was a car off the road, parked on the right. Again, no motor running and no lights until I passed, and it also followed me.

We were starting to approach a creek ahead. She emphasized strongly, "Don't stop. Keep going so you don't get stuck." I started down the muddy bank and across the soft bed of the creek, praying I wouldn't get stuck. I stepped on the gas and made it up the other side. My heart was pounding out of my chest! I was so relieved when I made it and was in a large grassy field.

We arrived at a type of gathering, like a picnic. Next, we were inside sitting at a bar. There was a man sitting at the bar and he was intoxicated and depressed. He kept saying he wanted to see his child. I was having a conversation with his child and I kept saying, "He is right here in front of you." He couldn't see him. The child was holding on to the corner of the bar with both hands, but then slipped through the man's fingers. The man had no idea what had just happened. I kept telling him that his child was right there, just keep trying.

Devee was all about filling me in on everything and I knew she was my new Guide! She is so advanced as a Spiritual Guide and she has stepped in to lead this journey! She was on a bus and it was starting to pull away while I was running alongside, desperate for more insight from her.

When I woke up, I was hungry to learn more. I happen to have a book on Angels, Divinities, and Deities. I instantly opened it up and I found "Devee" or Devi—she is the female embodiment of God! I know her in the yoga world as Shakti.

It is always hard for me to grasp such a visit. I always go to, "Who am I to have such a high embodiment of Spirit to guide me?" This is a question I no longer need the answer for. I am fully open for the next chapter in my life as a Medium! She told me of the levels so I could understand we have an important journey ahead.

A Soul's Blueprint

One of my favorite chants to do in yoga is the Jaiya Jaiya. It was explained to me by a yoga teacher years ago. It was my understanding that the "Divine Mother" is cradling us in her lap and wrapping her arms of unconditional love around us! So as we chant it, this is exactly what I feel. She is referred to as Devi in the chant. Now I fully see! Spirit has a way of laying out the groundwork during our lifetime so we can uncover the golden nugget of life!

What I am sure of is Devi came to me so she can teach me to help others heal their grief through compassion and to heal their Souls! She also told me she sent me my dogs Rocky and Willow because they are full of unconditional love and healing. They, too, are my teachers.

My strongest connection to Devi is in nature as she helps to detox my body and Soul! From my understanding, the Jaiya Jaiya chant meaning is "Celebrating the Divine Mother, Creator, and Nurturer in the Universe." It is us paying homage to her as we chant it. It is in honor of her and aligns us with her, which is the very essence of all that is good and auspicious!

Photo by Lacey Matthews

Chapter 13

GHOST ... SPIRITS ... WHAT?

Loren's Story

As I enter in my second decade as lead investigator for the American Hauntings paranormal tour company, it's safe to say I have run across many mediums, sensitives, psychics, or whatever the topical term for a forecaster these days is. That along with my "pays the bills" occupation in Law Enforcement has not only made me skeptical, but a harsh critic as well.

I have traveled the country and met quite a few "prophets" that dealt with generalities. When giving a reading, insights and predictions are transferred that could apply to hundreds, if not thousands, of people in our society. Despite all my personal negativity, there are times that I do ask a few to come along with me on investigations. Give the public what they want, right? Good business practice, right?

I had heard of Cheryl Kearns and her daughter Lacey Matthews for a while. Jacksonville is so small, how could you not? Honestly, most of the time, I brushed it off as "been there, done that." I just wasn't interested until I heard of the peace and closure they provided a mutual friend after the tragic death of a family member. This was about the same time that I was preparing for a paranormal class I periodically teach for Lincoln Land Community College. A non-credit "Ghosthunting 101," if you will. I try to cover everything from basic beliefs to photography to state-of-the-art equipment in four short sessions. I contacted Cheryl to ask if Lacey and she would be interested to come as guest speakers—to which they accepted, thankfully.

This was my first time meeting these two beautiful, personable ladies who answered question after question of the "how to" and "why" of what they do. I came away with a whole new appreciation and understanding of what it is that they live with. What you hear so many refer to as a gift, I feel Cheryl and Lacey see as an obligation: an obligation to bring healing and relief to those who aren't ready to say goodbye to a cherished loved one.

That could not have been more evident than later at a group reading I was invited to attend. A group of total strangers and I gathered upstairs at Inner Harmony Salon one afternoon to attempt to connect or reconnect to those who had crossed over, with assistance from Cheryl and Lacey. Those gathered had lost children, siblings, or parents, all in recent history. I noticed early on that both women were "doodling" on paper as they talked. I would learn later that this was Spirit writing or automatic writing. Sometimes there are words, but often just doodles as they received messages. I witnessed first-hand messages delivered to a few that had been long coming. These were personal messages of relief and contentment that neither of the ladies could have known prior. I also watched their display of compassion. When a personal message was a little too "close to home," they assured the receiver that message would be given to them later, privately. Too often in the past, I have seen psychics deliver messages to promote themselves with no regard for the privacy and dignity of the respondent. Not on this day. Everyone in the room was treated in the manner they would hope for. Not everyone was guaranteed a message, which I can respect and appreciate. I can't guarantee a ghost sighting on every investigation. We deal with the Spirit or left energy of the departed, not a puppet who performs on demand. Needless to say, no message for me that afternoon. That's okay. The living really don't want to communicate with me most days, why should the dead? Messages were received by those who truly had been waiting a long time to hear them, so fine by me. I also was observant to see how physically and emotionally draining these were on Cheryl and Lacey. To have some messages of despair and loss come at you without warning and at any hour of the day or night. A "gift," you say? Not in my book.

Finally, after this remarkable afternoon I encountered, I asked them to join me on a paranormal investigation. This was something I had been hesitant to do. You see, Cheryl and Lacey feel the obligation to send a Spirit into the light if needed. In my business, I'm out of work if that happens. That's a joke to anyone who just dropped the book. They accompanied me to the former Williamson Funeral Home, which is now the Jacksonville Dream Center. This century-old structure has seen many past lives. This is a location full of local history, but not television known paranormal history. And despite that, Cheryl and Lacey had picked up on many of the same dark secrets I have been unearthing there for over ten years. Again, subtle things that they could not have been aware of. To my knowledge, it was the first time either had entered the doorway. I take pleasure in boasting that I have gotten to know Cheryl and Lacey on a personal level and I'm the better person for it. I hope to work with them both at different locations for many years to come—I will be honored. I will say this to those on the fence of searching for a specific answer: be careful of what you ask for. You just might get it.

—Loren Hamilton

Williamson Funeral Home on Sandy Street

Lacey told me Loren Hamilton invited us to come to one of his Ghost Hunt Tours that he was doing for American Hauntings. It was across the street from my business, Inner Harmony, in Jacksonville at the old Williamson Funeral Home. I thought, "What the heck. It would probably be fun." Now keep in mind, we cross Souls over to the Other Side that are what we call, Earthbound Spirits. When we go to any haunted place, we never see negative Spirits. They are afraid we are going to cross them over. So our experience has been flat, to say the least.

We met Loren when he asked us to speak to his class that he was teaching on Ghost Hunting. I was excited to speak at it and Lacey was dragging her feet because of people's skepticism. She was not wanting to do it, but when we did, she took the lead and we really enjoyed telling our side of seeing Spirits.

When Loren asked us to join his Ghost Hunt, I thought we were just one of the many who joined for the experience.

When we were getting ready to go, Lacey said we better grab a bottle of water, flashlight, pendulum, and our journals that we use to record our readings. As we were walking over, she said we might want to take notes of what we see and experience. We sent a message to all of the Ghosts that we were just there to communicate, not cross anyone over. Loren still needs this gig, as I am laughing.

What I didn't know was at the end of the tour, Lacey and I were supposed to tell the group what all we picked up on. I find this extremely hilarious because I never figured it out until he asked us to speak at the end.

As soon as we arrived and were walking up the steps, Lacey said, "Mom, there is a Spirit of a man with dark hair in a black suit with a top hat." When we all gathered around and Loren started to tell us a little history about the building, I zoned out and was channeling a young woman, 32 or 33 years old, wearing a long white dress. I didn't hear anything Loren was saying because I was channeling her. He was standing by a pillar and he would rock his body back and forth. As he would do this each time, he rocked forward past the pillar, and she would blow in his ear. She was so playful and having a blast with this. I couldn't take my eyes off of her and I was trying to keep from bursting out in laughter.

Loren broke us up into three groups. Lacey and I were in a group together. As we walked around, we got many messages. So many Spirits there. We would walk in a room and tune in and listen. I had a young boy "J," Jay, or Jake (around eight years old) who came to me. I heard the song "Sherry Baby." So many Spirits and a lot of them did not have a happy experience to tell. One mom talked about being strapped down in a chair. I heard "Nut House" and "Electric Chair," and one either jumped out of the window and committed suicide or he wanted to: a lot of depression and heaviness. I had a man come through with a shorter left leg, prosthetic leg, or drop foot syndrome. One of the brighter parts was downstairs. I could hear a player piano playing. I kept humming this song because I couldn't think of the name of it. One of the other participants heard me, and said, "The Entertainer." "Yep, that's the song," I said.

Lacey even picked up on a bird that was there and other animals. There was a lot going on. When we went upstairs and slowly made our way room to room, Lacey approached a closet door and when she opened it, there was a very large portrait of the Spirit of the man with the dark hair, black suit, and top hat. We both gasped and said, "Wow! There he is"—the Spirit Lacey saw as we entered the building earlier.

There was a small dressing room upstairs and the energy there was very heavy. It made Lacey and me both very uncomfortable. We couldn't get out of that room quickly enough.

Lacey and I knew nothing about the history of this building so our exploration was organic and a lot of fun. We look forward to accompanying Loren on future Ghost Hunts, now that the Spirits know that we aren't there to cross them over. Thank you, Loren, for the opportunity to explore a different experience of Spirit.

Spooning

My best advice to you about this work is learn as much as you can so you have the "tools in your backpack of knowledge" to use when needed. I am so thankful that I dug in and took classes and studied all of this because if I hadn't, this next encounter would have freaked me out. Raymon Grace had taught me well on how to dowse. I think it all came easy to me, except your thoughts and desires can lead or change the outcome of your Dowsing results and give you a false answer because it was what you desired it to be.

I always ask that my desires and opinions be removed, as to not sway the outcome of the dowsing. It's hard to do, but your results are far more accurate. It's the same when we sit down to do a reading. You just become unattached to the outcome and it is completely organic at that point. In other words, it comes from Spirit, not from you.

I was asleep upstairs at my business. In the beginning, I would stay overnight at the business when the weather was bad or just to save gas money because I live 45 minutes away. I was in a sound sleep when I was so rudely awakened from a Spirit spooning me. When I am awakened from a sound sleep in the middle of the night, I am not happy. I was aggravated, to say the least. How dare this Spirit think it was okay to invade my personal space.

I sat straight up, turned on the lamp, grabbed my pendulum, and began to dowse. I asked if this Spirit was of love and light and got a BIG NO! I asked his name and got a first and last name. I asked Archangel Michael to remove him: Done! I called Raymon that morning to have him check to see if this was real and he confirmed it! Don't ever question your gut instinct. But it's always nice to get a second opinion.

I was grateful to have the knowledge and ability to remove this negative Spirit. Had I not known how to dowse and remove a Spirit, I might not have been so calm.

Plain Jane

The building I have my business in was built in the 1890s. It has accommodated many types of businesses over the years, leaving many imprints and past Spirits. To add to that, next door, which is attached to my building, was once a church. Many times, past Spirits that went to that church have not crossed over due to fear of where they will end up. You will find a variety of Spirits due to past history of the building or the ground it sits on. Also keep in mind that Spirits have a way of finding you when they find out you can communicate with them. It's sad to me when a Spirit gets stuck here, known as an "Earthbound Spirit," so my door is always open to help.

One early morning after I had spent the night at the business, I came downstairs to fix my hair. It was winter and I'm an early riser so it was still dark out. Of course, the street lights lowly lit the inside so I didn't turn on any extra lights. I leave a couple of floor lamps on all of the time so they gave me plenty of light to do my hair. It was peaceful and quiet as I turned my head upside down to blow dry my hair. As I finished and brought my head up at the hair station that I was using, I saw a 30-something-year-old female Spirit standing at my front desk. Her hair was long and very plain and drab; she wore a simple cotton skirt and top. She was very "Plain Jane." As I acknowledged her and she me, I asked her what I could do for her. She was kind of shy so I asked if she wanted help crossing over to the Other Side. She said, yes, she did. I began the process as I visualized the path and used my pendulum, but couldn't get her to cross. After several attempts, I gave up. Later I called Raymon and he could see her, and he began to talk to her. I heard him say, "No problem," as if she was upset. He crossed her over and told me she got a little upset with him when he asked her if she came to me because she heard I could help her and she told him, yes. He asked why she wouldn't let me cross her over. She told him she came to me to get him so he could do it. I laughed and said, "I would want someone experienced, too."

All I cared was that she crossed and wasn't hanging out at my business anymore.

Hardin Salvage Yard and the Alton Bridge Backwater

One day I was driving to St. Louis, Missouri for my monthly chiropractic visit. During these visits I would also receive energy work, card readings, etc. It took me two hours to make the trip. I always looked forward to the drive because it was very meditative for me.

I was about 45 minutes into my trip when I crossed the Hardin, Illinois bridge. After you cross the bridge, there is a junk yard on the right side of the road. I casually glanced over and saw a man in his thirties with thick black hair sitting in one of the junk trucks. I did a double take and he was looking right at me as if to say, "Do you see me? I see you!"

I knew what I saw, yet it surprised me because I really hadn't ever seen a Spirit 3D! I pondered it and thought maybe it was my imagination. I thought to myself, "I don't see Spirits." I didn't think much of it. I just kept driving and enjoying the sunshine coming through the window and the outside air blowing through the sunroof.

About thirty minutes later, I crossed the Alton bridge and to the right was the backwater. There were stumps of trees in the backwater, but what came next made my heart skip a beat.

I saw an Indian village burned to the ground. I saw and smelled smoke that was smoldering and there stood one lonely young Indian girl. She was in her late teens and she looked right at me. She had tears running down her face as she said to me, "White man did this!" She said she had gone to gather berries and when she returned, the village was burned to the ground and everyone was dead. I will never forget the pain I felt for her. I told her how deeply sorry I was as tears ran down my face.

I arrived at my appointment in St. Louis and told my doctor all about it. I told her I saw the man at the junkyard and the Indian girl at the bridge. I said maybe I just made it up. But I knew what I saw and what I heard. She told me not to question it. I never believed I would be one of "Those People" who saw, heard, or felt Spirit.

Not me. I'm nothing special. Only special people with the special gift of clairvoyance, clairaudience, clairsentience, or claircognianze could do that! You know the ones who are born with "the Gift." Definitely not me! I was always curious about these abilities, but it never even crossed my mind that I would someday be one of "Those People."

Savannah, Georgia

I think it was February, 2012 when my husband Ben and I went on a trip to Savannah, Georgia. I remember talking to Ben about us getting away and he said to ask around where a nice trip would be. I asked a lot of my hair clients, friends, yoga students, etc. I remember one of them suggested Savannah and, for some reason, I was drawn to it immediately.

I had no idea why, but that's where I wanted to go. I mentioned it in one of my yoga classes and one of my students replied, "You know that's the biggest ghost town in the U.S.!" I had no idea!

We decided to drive down and spend a few days. I was excited because I just knew I was going to see and communicate with so many ghosts! Much to my surprise that wasn't the case at all. When we first arrived and got settled, we made our way to one of the town squares. They had a horse-drawn wagon ghost tour and I thought, "You bet!" I just knew Spirit was going to flood me with sightings and messages.

It was unseasonably cold so after we ate I stopped in a shop to buy a shawl. I was so excited for the tour to start. It was finally time and we loaded up with six to eight other folks. The guide did an awesome job telling us the history of the town on the tour. We went by a cemetery, of course, and I thought I'd see something, but, nope. Nothing.

We passed the most haunted hotel/eatery. Again, nothing. Building by building, story by story, I saw nothing. Finally, at one of the last stops, Ben and I both felt this overwhelming sadness and despair. It was a building where in the upper story they had created a makeshift hospital for children dying of an epidemic illness. The parents would stand on the street and look up and talk to the kids. The nurses never turned off the lights because they didn't want the children dying in the dark. They say to this day, if they turn off the lights, the Spirits turn them back on!

About two weeks after we got home, I was in my breakroom at my business and glanced out at my work station. I saw a Mammie Spirit sitting in the dryer chair. I mentally asked her if she hitched a ride back with us and she said she did. She heard I helped Spirits cross over and wanted my help. So I helped her make it to the Other Side. A couple of days later, I was at my station and glanced back at the breakroom and saw a large, heavy-set Mammie. She needed the same help.

You never know how Spirit will approach you and in what manner you will be the conduit to help them. The thing I know is that I am so humbled to be here to help out.

As you see, I was expecting to see and communicate with them and it didn't happen. Then when I wasn't expecting it at all, it happened. You just have to know that Spirit knows best. Take what you get when you get it and be thankful.

Chapter 14

BE EXTRAORDINARY

My Kids and Spirits (by Lacey Matthews)

I never could have imagined the gift I was being given. From an infant, Malik would stare at the ceilings and laugh. He would look off somewhere and be so happy, as though he was interacting with someone (when I could see no one there). I later found out just how connected babies are with the Other Side. As my son started getting older, his abilities started showing themselves more and more. As a mother, I was protective of him—still am and always will be—but I was astounded at this miracle child of mine. How did I get so lucky to receive such a little blessing? I knew this gift would come with some big struggles and I wanted to shelter him from that. I might be a bit of a "momma bear" when it comes to my children. How does a parent protect their child from something they can't see? What I didn't realize then that I do now is that my son didn't need protecting. I was hiding from my gift so, therefore, I didn't completely understand it and wanted to protect my child from something that he completely understood. Again, just how crazy is life?

Malik had a few experiences with Spirits in our house in Florida. The day we realized just how significant his gift is was on our drive to Illinois on New Year's Day. At least this was the day I finally understood how special he is. You have to keep in mind that while we took this trip home there weren't many businesses open on New Year's Day. A while into our trip, Malik started getting sick. Malik was three and a half years old as we traveled to Illinois. He had never gotten sick in a car before and, without many options of places open, my mom climbed in the back with him and started dowsing. For those of you unfamiliar with dowsing, the best way I can describe it is like witching for water. You use a pendulum, crystal, bobber, anything really that swings, and everything is made up of energy so the energy moves the pendulum. Now for me, it's the Spirit Guides, Angels, and God that help it move and give answers. My mom started dowsing and she began to ask my three-and-a-half-year-old questions. Malik started telling us that there were negative Spirits in the car and where they were. I was blown away because after him telling my mom what and where they were, after dowsing to get rid of them and Malik confirming that they were gone, he felt much better. This was the moment I realized not only how much dowsing helped, but also the abilities my son had. We made it to Illinois, but not without life as I knew it changing significantly.

I want to give you a few more pieces of information regarding my son Malik's abilities. My husband and I have three children: Malik who is nine, Nevaeh who is five, and Kenyon who is three. Each of my children are complete and utter blessings! Malik is my tender-hearted, loving, and affectionate little Soul who has been blessed with the gift of being a Medium. Nevaeh is my little spitfire who keeps us on our toes and will give her daddy a heart attack when she starts dating. She can also communicate with animals living or deceased. Kenyon is my little monkey—literally! He is my daredevil and nothing fazes this child. He is 100% BOY! At this time, I am unsure what abilities Kenyon has or will have, but this child will give the world a wake-up call for sure. I have told you a little about when we realized Malik was a Medium, but let me get a little more in-depth as he plays a huge role in the events that unfolded.

Be Extraordinary

We moved to Illinois in January, 2008. In February of the same year, Malik started talking about this Spirit he called LaLa that appeared one day. Then shortly after, she was joined by Rogere and Rose. In second grade, Malik had to write a story for a school assignment and he wanted to tell the story of his three Spirits. Here is his story:

Lala, Rogere, and Rose are ghosts. I am the only one who can see them. They can pick up a ghost ball. They all have jobs to do. They like to play a lot of the things I like to play.

Lala came to me first. She has long blonde hair, green eyes, and light skin. She died when she was 92. She died of old age. Her birthday is on Halloween, October 31. She died 12 years ago. Lala has lots of friends in Heaven. She was not married and had no children. Her favorite color is red, just like me. I saw Lala first when she came through the ceiling in my room. She didn't know I had a fan and she about threw up on me!

Rogere came to me second. He had short black hair, blue eyes, and light skin. He's almost as strong as my daddy. He always beats me at arm wrestling. I never win! He was 93 when he died. He died of old age. He died 3 years ago. He had no children and no wife. He came through my back door and he saw our kitchen, living room, my sister's room, Mom and Dads' room, and then my room. He didn't know anyone was living here. He didn't know our names until I told him. When my brother was born, I told him because there wasn't enough room in the car for him to go. He is staying here because he doesn't have a home. He really likes football and the Chicago Bears are his favorite, just like my daddy! Rogere's birthday is December 25.

Rose came to me last. She has long red hair, dark brown eyes, and light skin. Her birthday is November 21. She died when she was 40 years old. Someone shot and killed her in her backyard while she was planting flowers and food by her swing. She died 30 years ago. She was very sad when she got killed. She came through the garage wall and got burnt on our living room lamp. She didn't know where to go. She came to my room and ran and jumped on my bed. She didn't know I was in it. I said "Hi, what is your name?" She likes pizza, like me!

They all sleep in bed with me. I share my pillows and blankets with them. Sometimes while they are on the bed, they accidentally push me off of it. Lala, Rogere, and Rose think my baby brother is cute! We play together a lot. It's not the time for them to go to Heaven right now. One day they want me to help them get there. This is my story of myself, Lala, Rogere, and Rose.

—Malik 1-15-11

We were all blown away with his ability. Malik later found out from the help of my mom—Nana to Malik—that these are his Spirit Guides, their names, what they look like and more, but he never realized these three were his Spirit Guides. After he asked them why they never told him, they responded by saying he needed to figure it out. Spirit Guides are really good at not giving information until we need to know it. To most people, seeing Spirits would be a scary or uncommon event, but to Malik it is normal everyday life. He constantly teases me about being afraid to see Spirits and reminds me it is not scary at all. From the mouths of babes!!

Even with all of us on this already incredible journey, none of us knew what was to come, the doors that would be opened, or how drastically life would change in the blink of an eye. My mom and I are able to communicate and have the ability to cross Spirits over, Malik is a Medium, Nevaeh can communicate with animals. This was life as we knew it at the time.

We talked to our friend Raymon and told him about the kids' abilities to communicate with Spirit and he suggested that I do an interview with them. So I took his advice and am glad I did. I was amazed at the outcome.

An Interview with Malik (Age 9)
"Meet His Spirit Guides"

Rogere—Kentucky
- Five lives
- Jobs: pilot, mountain climber, wrote books
- Lessons learned: don't treat others mean and don't be a bully, follow the rules
- Life #2: born when George Washington died (December 14, 1799)
- One life born after the Civil War (1865)
- Died due to asthma in one life at age 28
- Lived once to be 80
- Lived once to be 59, died on his birthday

Lala—New York
- 31 lives
- Jobs: hairstylist, knitter, stuffed pillows, made jewelry, wrote lots of books but never sold them
- Lessons: be kind, don't trick people because they then won't believe you (learned those lessons in her first two lives)
- She only remembers six of her lives
- Lived to 93 in one life (1973)
- She got shot when she was 19
- Died of dehydration (because she wanted to see how long she could live without water) (Malik said she was really dumb back then!)

- One life was when Abe Lincoln was President (1861-1865)
- She got ran over by a car because she wasn't looking
- Died when Thomas Jefferson's President years were over (1809)

Rose—lived in Texas but moved when she was two to New York
- Eight lives
- Lessons learned: treat everyone fairly, don't cheat, be nice to everyone, don't argue with a cop
- Jobs: circus (blew up balloons), made picture frames, pilot one year but quit because she didn't like it, actress, football player, teacher
- Born when soccer started in the United States (1901)
- Died when baseball became popular in the United States (1791)
- She died at 30 and the telephone was invented right after her death (1876)
- Born on the first-ever Halloween (1500) (United States 1840)
- She was a witch in one life
- She's here because not a lot of people can see her and hear her. Wants to be crossed over in a couple of years. She's waiting on her brother to cross over. He told her when he was going to be crossed over so she wants to wait until he crosses over. She doesn't know why he is waiting. He's going to cross over in New York in 2018.
- Some ghosts know how to vanish and not be seen.
- All the ghosts she works with need to be crossed over but they can wait only 100 years if they want to.
- Sometimes ghosts have a hard time crossing over so they search for people who can see them.

An Interview with Nevaeh (Age 5)
"Meet Her Spirit Guides"

Robin (boy)—Bulldog
- Five years old when he died
- Two lives
- Got killed by a super hard small knife

Gracie—Puppy
- Five lives
- 13 when she died (two years ago)
- Got shot by a guy who didn't like puppies with blonde fur
- Gracie goes to school for teenagers

Robert—Zebra
- Eight years old when he died
- November 18 birthday
- Seven lives
- Hit his head and poked his eye
- They play with toys!
- They saw Nevaeh when she was four and saw her teaching fairies and thought she would be good with ghosts also.

Lacey Teaching

On July 30, 2012, I was laying in my hammock watching my children play in the yard. My oldest son Malik came and sat down and we started talking about what Spirits he had seen lately. He told me there was a Spirit of a little girl behind me. He said she told him she was lost. So I walked him through the process of crossing her over. We went for a walk to the Medicine Place to meet my Spirit Guides to take her to the light. Malik talked to her the entire time, repeating everything I said, reassuring her that she was safe. Then he asked her to go to the light. Then he asked her if there was a family member who had crossed over that she would like to meet. She responded with wanting to meet her mother. They reunited and my Spirit Guides walked them through the tunnel of light. After we got back from our meditative walk, Malik decided he wanted to meet his Spirit Guides and I promised to get the Medicine Place CD of Raymon Grace so he can meet his Spirit Guides. So this is the next on my to-do list for him.

Out of the Mouths of Babes

My youngest child Kenyon was only three years old when Leo passed. One day we were headed out to go shopping and decided to stop by to visit Leo's grave. After we paid our respects and were getting ready to leave, I told Kenyon to tell Leo goodbye. He looked at Leo's picture on the headstone of the mausoleum and said, "That's not the real Leo!" Then I saw him look off to the side. He looked at me and then back at the mausoleum and said, "Bye Leo's picture!" Then he looked off to the side and waved at him and said, "Come on Leo, let's go shopping." I literally stopped and smiled as we walked away!

At such a young age, everything is so clear between a child and Spirit! One day I was taking a bubble bath and Kenyon came in. After a few minutes he said, "Mommy, Leo's here and he is popping your bubbles." I said, "Tell him to stop popping my bubbles!" Kenyon laughed and said, "Aww, Leo loves his mommy, like I love my mommy."

To this day, I am grateful to Raymon for suggesting I interview my kids. The information is priceless. As kids grow older and go through puberty, they can lose their connection to the Other Side while they are growing up and just being kids. Malik and Nevaeh don't remember these connections to Spirit but Mom and I know that they will reconnect in the future if they so desire.

As for Kenyon at age eight, he sure is handy to call in our "Parking Angels" when we need a good parking spot.

My Grandkids
"Dance Recital"

I was driving to Nevaeh and Kenyon's dance recital in May, 2014 and called Tonia. I could tell Spirit was with me, but I wasn't connecting who it was. I had a nice conversation with my friend. We talked about us going to Italy together one day. We have had this conversation several times since I opened Inner Harmony back in 2006, but it has never seemed to be the right time for us to go. She is going this summer, 2014, a year after Leo passed. She goes on a Spiritual Pilgrimage walk that she always looks forward to and spends time with her dad. Morgan's aunt and Tonia's good friend are going with her on the walk. Tonia and I always have a wonderful conversation when we talk on the phone or get together. I am sure Leo brought us back together for the very reason that he would be able to talk to his mom and dad through me. I am still amazed at the Mother's Day card he gave his mom about a month before his passing. He wrote in the card "You need to spend more time with Cheryl!" His Spirit already knew what was coming.

At the recital, my six-year-old granddaughter Nevaeh was in four numbers and Kenyon, age four, did one tumbling class. As I watched her first dance, it brought tears to my eyes. I remember her mama, Lacey, when she was that age. She was so sweet up there on the stage that night. Next came Kenyon for his tumbling debut. Kenyon is so funny and he takes the world by storm. The class came out and did a forward roll and then scooted off the stage. Next, they took turns tumbling down the ramp. He couldn't quite make it up the ramp by himself so the teacher helped him up and he rolled off the side as we all laughed. He got back on the ramp and did his rolls wonderfully. We all cheered for him.

After the recital, I rode back to the kids' house and then headed home. I was just outside of town when Leo and Morgan popped in. Now I know who the Spirit was that I felt earlier. You would think since Leo is one of my Spirit Guides that I would recognize him immediately, but that wasn't the case that night. What I'm about to tell you next will clear that up for you.

Spirit gives me the space I need with family events and things that are near and dear to my heart. Leo knows how much I enjoy my family so he had made his presence known while I was talking to his mom, but not revealing his identity. As Mediums, we need to be taken off guard with our messages, especially when it is a Spirit that we know very well. The message is so much more powerful and meaningful that way: organic, if you will.

As I drove out of town, Morgan (whom I'd only channeled a couple of times) came through with Leo. He was on the floor belly laughing as he showed me Kenyon rolling off the ramp and he told me that he was just like Kenyon as a child—bigger than life! Morgan was with Nevaeh, stroking her braids and talking about how beautiful she is. They told me that they are watching over Lacey's kids, protecting them. It was important to Leo for me to tell his mom Tonia that.

The next thing that they showed me brought tears to my eyes. They took me to the wreck site where they died. I told them that this wasn't what I wanted to see, but they insisted that it was very important to their families to hear. I was with them on the motorcycle and Leo showed me at impact that he put his arms around Morgan to protect her. He and Morgan were lifted and doing forward rolls like Kenyon did in the recital. They were dressed in white shirts, and they needed their families to know that they did not experience the crash. How Leo told me was, "It was like 'Star Trek.' 'Beam me up Scottie!'" Their Spirits knew exactly the plan. They were safe and at peace, even at the wreck sight. Next, Leo took me to the funeral home and we stood at the head of his casket. He commented on the fact that some of his extended family cut in line and that he didn't think that was cool. He was standing there when his mom told me, "Look at him Cheryl. He just looks like he is sleeping." I told Leo I felt like I could pass out. He let me know we were fine and to be strong for his family.

This was all hard for me to see, but as I wiped the tears from my eyes, I realized that he needs his mom and dad and Peter and Filie to know that they are at peace with it all and are always around them.

This message was very hard for me to tell my friend. I don't like going to the scene of the wreck or the funeral home, but it was important to Leo so I delivered the message. Leo's family drives past the wreck site every day because it is on their way to and from work. It is also on the way to our apartments that we bought from Sam and Tonia. Lacey does photography on the side and likes to go out to the apartments and take photos outdoors. She was on her way out there a week ago and at the intersection where the accident happened, two birds flew in front of her car and they did on the way back home, also. The funny thing is, one just floated by and the other dive bombed her. I'll let you decide which one was Leo and which one was Morgan. They are too cute!

Spirit Through a Child's Eyes

I wish I knew then what I know now, would apply here. If we only realized that when a child is talking to what we think is an imaginary friend, it is really Spirit from the Other Side, we could have learned a lot. What you're about to read in this chapter just might make you change your mind. It is often the era and the way we are brought up that forms us into a belief system that might be a bit cloudy. I believed as you might have that we cannot communicate with Spirit and told as a child that it was wrong.

The innocence of a child should be enough to make us at least question it. Thank goodness I now not only pay attention and believe, but I take notes and truly listen. Sometimes a child is talking to one of our loved ones such as a grandparent who you were close to. As you listen, ask them to describe what they look like and if it sounds like your loved one, show them a picture. I know what you are thinking. They never met your loved one on this earth in the flesh, but trust me, they have met and interacted with them on the Other Side. What a gift this child and your loved one are trying to give you!

Have an open mind and open heart and let Spirit be your guide. We are blessed with the innocence and love of a child. Be still and listen as they reconnect you to those you yearn to be with again. The children are our guides and teachers. May we be humble and kind as we learn from them!

Chapter 15

A TIME TO HEAL

Embrace the Journey

As I sit to bring this book to a close, I realize it's just going to be a pause. As you have read and witnessed the healing that Spirit has brought to those who have shared their stories, my hope is that it has opened your heart to the power of healing that you can receive from a reading. The prayer I prayed and conveyed to God as a child, "If only I had a hotline to God," came true. As Lacey and I sit down to do a reading, we are blessed to know we have that so-called Red Telephone to Spirit.

I want to leave you with these next two stories so Spirit can wipe away any remaining doubt you might have. It's your "Free Will" to journey down this path of possibilities and decide for yourself. For me, I know that God, the Angels, our loved ones, and Spirit are my lighthouse beacon that is guiding Lacey and me as "Inner Harmony Mediums" to deliver as many messages of healing as we can. Forever etched in my heart will be the day I found my "Paper Plate Angel." I know exactly who had my back, my saving grace: Spirit. I believe in the power of Spirit and cherish the many paths that Spirit has taken me down to get to this one.

When Lacey and I did the next two readings that you are about to read, they changed our life paths and we now joyfully embrace our paths as "Inner Harmony Mediums!"

One night after work as I was headed home, I checked my messages. There was a message from Apryl that simply said she had finished her story for my book. I think through life we all have those moments when Spirit speaks to us, guides us, nurtures us, heals us, and comforts us. Many times we simply dismiss it as coincidence. When you read Jared and Rachel's story, that's one of those moments, one of those so-called coincidences, but now we know it's not coincidence—it's Spirit connecting us to help us grow. When will we stop? When will we listen? And when will we open our Souls and act on it? I began to read Apryl's story and as I was reading, my body tingled with goosebumps with that signal that Spirit was opening my heart for a message. When I was about three-fourths of the way through her story, tears ran down my face and I was sobbing because it touched me so deeply. As I was crying, Leo came through and he simply said, "Cheryl now you know why you had to write this book!"

Jared and Rachel's Story
"There Are No Coincidences"

One Tuesday evening about 9:00 in the Fall of 2013, after Cathy and I had gotten together to do our dowsing, she said her daughter Rachel's husband Jared wanted a reading. Jared and Rachel miscarried a baby boy on Thanksgiving Day of 2009 and he was still struggling with the loss. Cathy had told the kids about me doing readings and Lacey doing card readings.

I told Cathy to give them a call to see if they wanted to come in for a reading. My heart just breaks when I hear about the pain someone is in over the loss of a child. She called them and they came up immediately.

I took Jared in by himself first. Their son Wyatt came through strongly. He told his daddy, "Don't cry, Daddy." Wyatt was with Jared's Grandpa Harvey. They were on a playground in Heaven. Wyatt talked about how he only came for a short visit, which referred to the miscarriage. He told Jared he was around him all the time. Wyatt can feel his daddy's pain of his heart. He is sad that his dad can't see him, but he said, "If Daddy can have 'still moments,' he will be able to see me."

Wyatt talked about the hair on Jared's leg. Jared said one month before, he felt his leg hair being touched, just out of the blue. That was Wyatt! Jared had it happen several times. We both had a good laugh over that.

Wyatt said he is at all of the birthday parties! He likes taking piggyback rides on Daddy as much as he can.

He then showed me that Jared's heart shattered to pieces after the loss. Wyatt was picking them up and putting a bandage on his heart with a big bow.

He said the doors are closed to Heaven and he was opening them so Daddy and his brother and the baby that Rachel is pregnant with could come play and jump in the leaves. I saw Grandpa as he rubbed Wyatt's head! What a sweet moment.

We finished up and Jared said, "Hey, what about the card reading?" I said that was Lacey's area. I could tell he wasn't going to drop it. I hesitated and then made the phone call to Lacey, with my fingers crossed.

Lacey answered the phone and I said, "So what are you doing?" She said, "I'm sitting here in my PJs." I told her what Jared said and she replied, "I'm not dressed." We said, "Come as you are," and she did!

She took Jared straight back to her room for the card reading and I took Rachel in for her reading. Lacey and I never spoke except for hello. We never talked about Jared's reading.

As soon as I sat down with Rachel, her Shih Tzu, Chili, that had passed at 15 years old came through. He was very excited about the baby. Next, Spirit said, "Stool, name on the bottom." At the time, we had no idea what this meant. A couple of years later I was needing something to set a plant on at my business and Cathy said I have the perfect stool for you. She mentioned to Rachel that she was going to give me this stool. Rachel immediately burst into tears. She said, "You can't give that to Cheryl. That was Grandma Fran's and she even signed it!" Cathy and I had no idea until now as we were looking at the reading notes—the infamous "Stool with the name on the bottom." Mystery solved! This was the stool in Rachel's reading.

Rachel's Grandma Carolyn came forward and spoke about a glass bell that they have. She also talked about an Angel figurine that her daughter gave Rachel in memory of her grandma. She also shared about the birthstone ring she and Grandpa had given Rachel. Rachel was very close to her Grandma Carolyn and was very happy that she came through at the reading.

Wyatt was jumping up and down because he was so excited to talk to his Mommy. He told her how happy he is and talked about being on Daddy's back. He told her all the stories about the playground with all of them there. He was blowing her kisses and said, "Daddy needs much healing." He knew Mommy was going to be okay. I think we were both wiping tears.

Wyatt said to respect "big brother" and Logan and baby Ronin can come play. He told her about a birthmark. When Ronin was born, he had a slight birthmark. Wyatt loves his brothers and parents and wants them to come play with him on the playground. He gets even more piggyback rides from his Uncle Adam who is in Heaven with him also!

Wyatt says he is a bright light with blonde hair like Logan. He says he is too cute as he kisses his Mommy's face and hooks his arms around her neck and says, "I see you."

When Rachel was little, she had a favorite blanket. They had tried to take it away, but she would pitch a fit. She wouldn't even let them wash it. One day it disappeared. Rachel's brother Adam, in Heaven, laughed about taking Rachel's blanket. He showed us, holding it by the corner because it was stinky. Rachel loved that blanket, but Adam had to take it away!

Now the conclusion to these readings is quite comical. When we finished, we all met in the kitchen and Jared looked at me and said, "What the F_ _ _?" I said, "What happened?" He pointed to Lacey and said, "She just told me the same thing you told me!" That was the deciding factor that Lacey said we needed to do the readings together. It wasn't long before Lacey and I started doing readings together as Inner Harmony Mediums! And so the story goes!

Apryl's Story
"Phone Calls to Heaven!"

It's 3 a.m. I am doing the exact same thing that I have done at 3 a.m. for the past 11 weeks. I am holding my infant son while his twin sister is fast asleep. My son is smiling at the chair in the corner of the living room. Some may say he is staring at a light, some may say it is just gas, but I know in my heart he is having a conversation with his papa. If his papa were here on earth with us, he would be sitting in the chair holding his grandson because that was HIS chair.

Let's back up, because that is not where the story starts.

In 1992, my mom got remarried and I gained my bonus dad. While some just gain a step-dad when their mother remarries, I gained a bonus dad. He worked with my "real" dad to help raise me. He attended every sporting event, made me breakfast, checked on my grades, and loved me as his own.

In 2003, I married my best friend. My bonus dad walked me down the aisle with my real dad. Both of my dads had a friendship and that made my life a lot easier. They could be in the same room at the same time, they could talk about my behavior and my previous boyfriends. They put me first.

In 2004, my husband and I decided we were ready to start a family. It didn't come easy for us. We were not successful. In 2008, my bonus dad was diagnosed with cancer. My husband left his career and started over so we could move back home. In 2009, we decided to do fertility treatments. Our insurance didn't cover the treatments and I was devastated. My bonus dad came to our house, sat in HIS chair and offered to pay for our first round of treatments. Sadly, they were unsuccessful.

In 2014, my bonus dad passed away. It was the most heart-wrenching experience I have ever been through. I told my bonus dad how much I loved him and I thanked him for everything. But I did have one selfish moment where I told him he couldn't leave us because I needed him to be a papa to my future kids. He sighed great big when I said those words and I live in forever regret for being so selfish.

After my bonus dad's passing, some of my friends mentioned Inner Harmony Mediums (Cheryl and Lacey) to me. A few weeks later, my mom, two of my sisters, and I had an appointment.

Our loved one came through. He had been watching us. He knew what was going on. He knew our pain. It was so comforting to know that he has been with us all along. Cheryl and Lacey told us things that NO ONE would have ever known. Pa was really talking to them. They gave us peace on some questions we had regarding his path and they gave us direction on how to handle some family issues. They even used terms and phrases that my Pa always used. He really was with us.

We continued to visit Cheryl and Lacey every six months or so. It was like a phone call to Heaven. It helped us with the grieving, it helped us make decisions, and it helped us heal. We were talking to our loved one. I can't describe to you the state of depression I would have been in if I didn't have that phone call to Heaven. I, along with my family, would have never been able to heal. We are at peace. We miss him every day, but we are at peace.

In 2017, my husband and I decided to do fertility treatments again. We had new insurance so we were covered. During our journey, my aunt passed away and also our beloved dog. For any couple experiencing infertility, you can understand how important their first dog was.

Our dog was 16; she was our first baby. Losing her was painful. I immediately called Cheryl and Lacey, just like I did when we lost our aunt. They were all booked up. But they knew how much pain I was in and offered to come in early for 30 minutes to help me. Yes, pets come through. Pa was there to greet my sweet baby. She wasn't alone and that is what I needed to hear. Once again, they gave me peace on things that occurred during her passing. They even explained that another dog would enter my life soon and my dog was okay with it. My dog was giving her to me. Two months later, our rescue came into our life. She was a hot mess and needed a lot of love. She filled the empty places in my heart.

In August, 2017, I learned we were finally pregnant. Finally! I didn't have a minute to enjoy it before the panic started. I am a very anxious person and I worry a lot. I was ten weeks into the pregnancy when I met with Cheryl and Lacey. I couldn't enjoy my pregnancy. I was worried too much. I was too scared of losing the babies. I hadn't touched my stomach, I hadn't talked to the babies, I wasn't excited. I waited 14 years for these babies and I was too scared to enjoy it.

Cheryl and Lacey gave me hope. They explained they do not and cannot predict the future. Anything can happen, but what they could tell me was that my pa, my aunt, and my sweet dog had all met the babies. They loved on them. Cheryl and Lacey saw horns and trumpets and to them that meant the pregnancy would be a success and I would be holding my babies in my arms. Cheryl and Lacey also cleared my energy so that I could feel peace. This helped me lessen my anxiety and actually enjoy my pregnancy. I felt so at ease and relaxed.

It is now 4 a.m. I am sitting in HIS chair, thinking about how much Cheryl and Lacey helped me heal. I could have visited a grief counselor, I could have taken antidepression medication, I could have made the choice not to get out of bed. I am not judging anyone who makes those choices—no choice is right or wrong. However, those phone calls to Heaven allowed me to continue with my life and it allowed me to be happy. It allowed me to remember the good times with my pa. It allowed me to adopt a new dog and it allowed me to enjoy my pregnancy. I wouldn't have made it through the last four years without their support. My son is named after his papa and I know they may have never met here on earth, but they already have a bond that I can't describe.

I want to publicly thank Cheryl and Lacey for their support. Without them, I wouldn't have been able to see the other side of grief. They truly help people heal and build relationships with their clients as they help them with their sadness.

–*Apryl*

Lacey Matthews and Cheryl S. Kearns (Photo by Melanie Miller)

ABOUT THE AUTHOR AND HER DAUGHTER
aka "INNER HARMONY MEDIUMS"

Cheryl S. Kearns and her daughter Lacey Matthews work together at Cheryl's Inner Harmony Day Spa/Salon and Healing Center in Jacksonville, Illinois. Cheryl is a stylist, business owner, and yoga teacher. Lacey is a massage therapist, photographer, and artist.

Cheryl and Lacey are now Intuitive Mediums. Spirit had a plan for these two to step out of their boxes and deliver healing messages from those who have crossed over to the Other Side to their loved ones here on earth.

Inner Harmony Mediums provide private, small, and large group readings.

Website | innerharmonymediums.com

Facebook | Inner Harmony Mediums

Inner Harmony Mediums | 227 S. Main Street | Jacksonville, Illinois 62650

Photo by Lacey Matthews

Cheryl S. Kearns and Lacey Matthews (Photo by Melanie Miller)

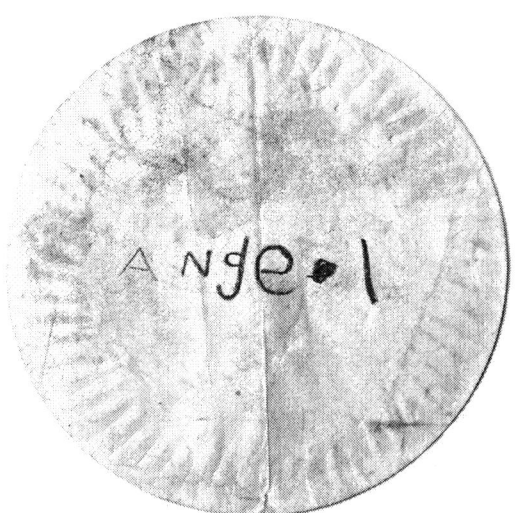

Paper Plate Angel (Photo by Melanie Miller)

Made in the USA
Columbia, SC
05 August 2019